A Little Bit of Nothingness

Eighty-One Observations
on the Unnameable

A Little Bit of Nothingness

Eighty-One Observations
on the Unnameable

Karl Renz

www.AperionBooks.com

APERION BOOKS™
1611A South Melrose Dr. #173
Vista, California 92081
www.AperionBooks.com

10 9 8 7 6 5 4 3 2
First edition
Printed in the United States of America

ISBN-10: 0-9829678-9-6
ISBN-13: 978-0-9829678-9-8
Library of Congress Catalog Card Number: 2012936180

English translation by Michèle Brehl

Cover & book design by CenterPointe Media
www.CenterPointeMedia.com

The world is a spiritual thing
that cannot be improved.
The one who tampers with it, damages it,
the one who wants to grasp it, loses it.
—TAO TE CHING

Contents

Foreword

Something Always Understands

What is man in his essence? What is the point of this whole existence? Is there a deeper meaning behind everything? These are the leading questions that have shaped our culture—religion, philosophy, science, and art—for thousands of years.

In this book we encounter Lao Tsu, a Chinese wise man who lived 2,500 years ago, and Karl Renz, a German artist and mystic of our time. They meet where time and space no longer have any meaning.

Lao Tsu is not a name but a title of honor, which means "The Elder." The transmission says that an old civil servant, who served as an archivist of scriptures, was leaving the empire when he was asked by a border patrol official to write down his realizations. Lao Tsu handed over more than 5,000 Chinese characters and continued on his way westward. The work influenced the governments of several later emperors and received the title *Tao Te Ching*, which roughly means "the classical book of the meaning of life."

There are many, often contradictory accounts, about Lao Tsu (Laozi) and the origin of the *Tao Te Ching* (DaodeJing). Equally diverse are the translations and interpretations that have spread across Europe since the nineteenth century. For this book, the German translation of Richard Wilhelm has been referenced, except for a few rare cases in which Rudolf Bachofen's translation was used.

Richard Wilhelm points out in his introduction that the term "Tao" is to be considered more like an "algebraic sign" for something that is fundamentally undefinable and unpronounceable. Tao has also been translated as "God," "the inscrutable," "the way," or as "sense" by Wilhelm Reich. In this book, it is simply referred to as Tao.

The idea to bring together the *Tao Te Ching* with some of the dialogues of Karl Renz comes from Dietmar Bittrich, the publisher of *Das Buch Karl* (published in English as *The Myth of Enlightenment*). In Karl's meetings, which he occasionally calls "Self Talks" or "Performances," he speaks completely spontaneously. Even he says that he doesn't know what speaks through him or what he speaks about. These transcribed recordings only very rarely refer to specific texts of the *Tao Te Ching*. This is more about an allocation and mutual fertilization of Karl Renz and Lao Tsu.

Karl addresses exactly that dimension of the Tao which is not graspable and usable. The rejection of how we function, in an organized and goal-oriented world, is a central theme that runs through the *Tao Te Ching,* while on quite another level through the talks of Karl Renz.

While Lao Tsu occasionally strives to enlighten the population and the empire through ethical principles, Karl's talks completely transcend ideas of "good" and "bad." But, as with many differences, they are only apparent. This unique combination darkens and illuminates, confuses and clarifies. One doesn't have to *understand* anything, but as Karl says, "Something always understands!"

—Christian Salvesen

Acknowledgments

Thanks to Michèle Brehl for her English translation from the original German, and to Adi Pieper for providing the initial editing.

Further assistance was given by Anasuya Hourdebaig and Konstantin Kravchuk.

1

The Tao That Can Be Named Is Not The Eternal Tao

This is already too much.

The Tao that can be named is not the eternal Tao.
"Non-Being" I call the beginning of heaven and earth,
"Being" I call the mother of individuals.
Both are one in their origin
and differ only in name.

What can be said *about* the Tao can't *be* the Tao. No matter how you define it: finite, infinite, present, absent, I, I-less, Being, That, or whatever, it will never fit.

You could as well say the word "underwear." For me, underwear fits best. This (pointing) is the coat and the underwear is always underneath. There, is what doesn't exist. It's existence that doesn't have to exist in order to exist. This is a paradox which also is when it isn't.

These are all just words pointing to something that doesn't need a pointer. All paradoxes you create are for the birds. Thank God.

Whatever you may say is already one sentence too many, but you might as well say it because everything is a lie. If you say, "I only know that I don't know anything," it does not matter because it can never be right. Yet, this is virtually always right, and it would be fatal if it was actually seen just once—if it could be found and made right—if the peace you are could be found in the truth of a sentence or a realization.

Questioner
I've already experienced that "I" no longer exists. There was no one anymore, no "I am." There was no one who could refer to a "me." Everything was gone.

Karl
Well, that's beautiful! Nevertheless it was still a circumstance. You can describe it, but it is not that of which I speak. I am talking about that which doesn't *know* any circumstance.

You would prefer this circumstance of non-being to existence, right? You liked it. It was quite nice, no? But in the absence of the "me" there was still someone who registered it. No matter how vague or distant, this one is still too many. Even the non-defined one is still something that is defined.

When I speak of that which is your nature—the nature of Being—I mean that which is in "all" circumstances.

It is that which is awareness. When there is "I am" then it is "I am," and when there is the world, then it is the world. When I sit here and say, "I am that. I am always that which is," there is no one who experiences himself as something special in the absence of a me.

That which can be described, explored, lived, experienced, can't be it. That's all. Should we write a book about this? Absolutely not. But then, why not!

Being And Non-Being Create Each Other

That's fun!

Being and Non-Being create each other.
Heavy and light complete each other.
Long and short mold each other.
High and low reverse each other.

God has to realize himself completely and absolutely. He can't realize himself a little bit or just so-so. He can't, for example, only realize himself intelligently. He has to realize equal amounts of stupidity and wisdom, in this perfect balance. So there has to be an equal amount of love and hatred, equal amounts of truth and untruth, and the same amount of darkness and light. There is always perfect harmony in this polar appearance of God's realization.

As soon as you have become a relative object of "found" Being, you find yourself sometimes clever, sometimes stupid; good yesterday and bad today; beautiful in the evening, ugly in the morning. This madness exists about six billion times in the world.

The Indian sage Nisargadatta Maharaj once said: There was a time when I had fallen into the madness of being born and as a result created billions of others. Then, I experienced the "I am" as reality and wanted to pass it on to everyone. I thought they should experience it, too. But since the apparent realization that there is "nothing to realize," and that Being is eternally realized, there is neither me nor others. Therefore, there is no "I am" nor anyone to whom I could impart anything.

Questioner
When the body we call Karl Renz is gone, is there then nothing left?

Karl
Was there ever a body? You could only say there is an energy that transforms itself incessantly. But the energy is always the same, just the way it is here and now. Nothing ever happened. Through all these transformations nothing ever changed. Yet, this will always keep on changing; there will be absolutely no end. That which you call this body, which appears to be born, may turn into worms and bugs. But why should this bug you now?

What happens here is just entertainment of Being. Nothing has to come out of it. That's the fun. Fun is needed and where there is fun there also has to be seriousness. And where there is earnestness, there has to be "Ernst" (a German name). And where there is Ernst, there has to be Ernestine. And where there is Ernestine, Being may fall asleep out of boredom or it may jump into the air. It plays chess with non-Being, because where there is Being there has to be non-Being, matter and anti-matter, always in equal amounts—and neither of it. Being and non-Being cause each other. Be happy, you worm!

The Sage Acts Without Acting

God works without working.

By not favoring the goodliest,
one prevents the people from quarreling.
The Sage acts without acting,
and everything falls into place.

That which is consciousness, that which is energy, is the all-wanting. But it cannot want what it wants. There is no causality.

On the relative level it looks as if there is a cause and an effect. But there is only the movement that is complete in itself, which is without being. It happens without having emerged; it passes without having existed.

This is simply the spontaneity of realization. No one calculated it ahead of time. Every action in Being is spontaneous and blind. This is freedom, the freedom of Being. It never has a direction. Everything happens spontaneously, out of itself, without any reason. There is no necessity. There is no one to think it would be better one way or another.

Yet, everything is an absolute necessity, because if it wasn't that way, the Absolute wouldn't be absolute. And that which is absolute Being doesn't know what is better or worse. But in this absolute "not-knowing," whatever can be realized is realized.

This could be called "karmic consciousness"—an absolute action which reacts to itself. The active and the reactive are not different. That which creates the first bang creates endless echoes of itself. It is both the echo and the cause; it is the effect and that upon which it has an effect. There is no separation in this, no causality, only the connection between action and reaction.

God works without working.

The Tao Is Without Essence

The stuff out of which dreams are made.

The Tao is without essence,
detaching beings from their beingness;
abysmally deep it is,
the ground of all that is.

God is without essence. God doesn't know himself as
God or as not-God. Jesus said on the cross, "It is ac-
complished." Here, he and God are not different.

That which is love doesn't *know* love. Love is where
there is no lover and no beloved. It's where you are
what you are. The Self—or whatever you call God—is
that which you are.

Your nature cannot be found. Whatever you can find
you will lose again. But the beauty of your nature is
that you haven't lost it in losing it. In the same way,
you won't find it in finding it again. The idea of "having lost it" is a dream, and the finding it—as dreamlike and beautiful as it might be—is also just a dream.
A mere dream wedding. And in all this dreaming, you
remain the stuff out of which dreams are made. And
good luck finding that

The All Doesn't Know Love

In love with ideas.

The all doesn't know love,
it walks over everything,
as if it was nothing.

Love is that which doesn't *know* love. That which
thinks it could love is just an idea. And that which
thinks it knows what love is is also an idea. "Love is
just a word," said Johannes Mario Simmel (German
novelist). He could have been right there.

For every word which points to "there is no second,"
you can create a second—especially from the word
"love." You immediately associate it with two and then
hope to overcome duality. You start pondering, "Is this
a relative love? Can I also have the absolute, unconditional, unconditioned, perfect love?" Not as long as
you exist! You feel love as a longing to be home, and
this longing arises with the assumption that you exist
and that you need a home. But you *don't* exist.

And now the dilemma: "Love your neighbor as you
love yourself." Can you imagine what this means?
First, you need to find a self that you could love. In
not-finding that which you could love in yourself, you
love that which you can't find in the other. But watch
out: if you can't find yourself, then there is no other,

either. Then, there is only love—without you, without any other.

Until then, you will cherish dream relationships and delight and suffer from them. The relationship to yourself is also a dream relationship; it's the relationship to an idea. In truth, there is no second to which you could have a relationship. But there are a lot of ideas with which you could have a relationships. You are always only in love with ideas, you can't help yourself.

At one time it is the idea of relative love, at another time that of absolute love. If you fall in love with the latter, you want to quickly get rid of relative love so that you can enjoy the absolute one. This way, you will forget yourself out of love; you will betray yourself out of love; you will fall low out of love.

Whether welcomed or rejected, forgotten or remembered, kissed or betrayed, it is always just you. You are the lover, the loving, and the beloved. And you will not escape this love for yourself. Everything is a love affair with yourself. And this affair is perfectly still because you are still.

All this loving and betraying is not real. In this perfect stillness there is no "second" to be loved. There is absolutely only you. Absolutely loveless. There is not even "something," nor is there "nothing."

The Spirit Of The Valley Doesn't Die

Levels of Consciousness.

The spirit of the valley doesn't die
it is called the dark female.
The gate of the dark female,
is called the root of heaven and earth.
Uninterrupted and persistent,
it works without effort.

The realization of reality starts prior to any "person." The person is the last stage in the levels of consciousness, the lowest level. At the beginning there is the Father, which is pure awareness of that which is Adam. *Adām* means "primal soul" in Hebrew. With this everything starts. It's the first body of light, the first experience of Being as light.

The second experience is Eve, or life, or that which is consciousness—the "I am." This is still impersonal, but there already exists the male and female principle—the so-called awareness and the consciousness principle.

There is consciousness in its purest form, which is Being or pure consciousness. Then it exists as spirit consciousness, the "I-am" Consciousness." Out of these two a third one emerges: the body and the sense of "I." This is where the ego, the identified consciousness of the person, begins. It emerges out of self-fertilization, out of the self-penetration of pure Being and consciousness. All this happens spontaneously and effortlessly.

Even with all this, nothing "starts," which is the basic point. Neither before nor through the first awakening does anything happen. Because that, which is Being, is *prior* to waking up to what Being is. If no one wakes up with the first awakening, no one is born. In being conscious, in the experience of the spirit, no one is born. And that, which arises out of the connection between awareness and consciousness, is also not born.

In this so called process of creation nothing is created, nothing emerges, nothing is born—and this is the essence.

The Sage Doesn't Want Anything For Himself

Seven ways of how the Self realizes itself.

Heaven is eternal and the earth is lasting.
They are lasting and eternal,
because they don't live for themselves.
The Sage doesn't want anything for himself,
which is why he is complete.

Each morning, you first wake up as the experiencer, and then experiencing happens as space, as spirit. Next comes that which is experienced, including the body. Thus, first is the Father, which is pure consciousness. Second is Eve, which is the Holy Spirit, the "I Am." Third is the Son, which is mankind—"I am the world." In the evening, when falling asleep, the third (the person) falls off first, then the "I Am," and finally awareness.

The personal and the impersonal keep taking turns, and you can't change this by will. When you recognize this, both become empty because neither brings lasting happiness. Then both disappear and only awareness—that first "I"—remains. But even this is one "I" too many. It still presupposes something which evades each definition or explanation. This alone is unconditional Being, the perfect mystery of yourself, and not some sort of perception. And still "you are." This is pure existence, which has absolutely no idea of what it is or is not. Pure potential.

And out of this pure potential, out of this fourth state, you wake up to a new life, into the fifth—the one of pure Awareness; then into the sixth—the one of pure Consciousness; and then into the seventh—the one of the pure Man. And this is that what Jesus was: Absolute Father, absolute Spirit, and absolute Son or Man. Seven ways for the Self to realize itself.

If your nature is absolutely that which is, then it possibly goes boom . . . boom . . . boom, without interruption. Then you are that . . . and that . . . and that

. . . which is the closest you can come to the perfect statement "I am–that–I am."

But even this is still one statement too many.

8

The Highest Good Is like Water

There is only absolute stillness.

The highest good is like water.
　　The water's goodness is
　　　to serve all beings without dispute.
　　　　　It dwells in places that all people despise.
　　　　　This is why it is close to the Tao.

Everything is exactly the way it is, because Being has manifested this way and not differently.

To be that which you cannot not be—or better, what you are—absolutely before everything and nothing, destroys all concepts. With concepts one can look at things from endless angles and develop new and different concepts.

There is the illusion that the path of suffering brings you "there." That it nails you to Being through heaviness, depression, etc. But I say, "You can never suffer enough, and never be joyful enough, to become that which you are." That which is Being, what you are, does not become more or less through suffering or joy. Not through you and not through anyone else.

The Self is never enlightened nor is it non-enlightened. It always is—before all concepts of enlightenment or non-enlightenment. Whatever you say about it is only conceptual.

The only thing that is not a concept is the Self. Is there ever a moment in time when the Self is not realized? Realization means that consciousness, temporarily identified as a finite object, again knows Being as awareness.

In the fleetingness of a shadow world, consciousness behaves actively and reactively. You are not part of phenomena; you are that which is before, during, and after. In reality, nothing moves—there is only absolute stillness.

When The Work Is Done, Withdraw

Everything is spontaneous and blind.

To hold onto fullnes:
is not worth the trouble.
When the work is done, withdraw.
This is the Heaven's Tao.

You can remain in *samadhi* for thousands of years, but as soon as the "I am" arises again, and with it the body, the hunger for "this" returns.

First there is the experience of separation, then the experience of oneness may follow. But it always requires someone who experiences—someone who can be in a circumstance and at the same time is separate from that circumstance, in order to *be* at all. It always starts with the first circumstance, the one of separation. Then you may possibly reach the second, that of oneness, apparently through practice. Any kind of practice is already grace, because if the totality doesn't want it you can't even lift your pinkie, let alone sit down and meditate.

Everything happens by itself and not caused by your will. What you are—your nature—has no will; it can't have a will. You will never be able to decide onto what your attention falls, or how you realize yourself. Everything is spontaneous and unseen. You can only be what you are, despite "how you realize" and not because of it.

The world cannot satisfy you anymore. You are now sitting together with other unsatisfied ones, and you may experience, for moments at a time, that nothing will ever be satisfactory. Then, suddenly, there is the peace that you long for so much, peace that you never expected to be there.

This Is The Secret Life

You are also when you are not.

Can you develop your soul so that it embraces the
One without scattering itself?
Can you unify your strength
and reach the softness
so that you become like a little child?

To create and not own,
to act and not hold on,
to multiply and not control:
this is the secret life.

What was the question, "*neti, neti?*" It's the double
negation: not this, not that. When someone asks you,
"Do you want coffee," you say, "No, tea." [*neti*] That's
why they are called "Tea-betans." They always pray
. . . that there is no coffee. Did you ever drink "Buddha-
tea?" Then you will really ask for coffee afterwards!

Neti, neti means, that which you are you cannot *not*
be. You are, now and here, no-when and no-where else.
You also *are* when you don't perceive this.

You have the experience of being, of being-ness, of
movement, of aliveness, of whatever. But in deep sleep
there is no experience at all. And do you not exist
then? Also when you don't know—prior to the "I-am"

perception—whether you are or not, you still exist!

For there to be an experiencer at all you have to be *prior* to the experiencer. So you also exist even when "this one" doesn't exist.

This is also without any experience; you *are* even when "you" are not.

That Which Is Not Serves The Work

The everywhere: It never moved.

Thirty spokes surround a hub;
therefore, nothingness constitutes the vehicle's work.
That which is serves ownership.
That which is not serves the work.

The absolute interrelation of Being is timeless and spaceless. It is time-and space-equal, always and everywhere, now and never, here and there, nowhere and everywhere—they are all one and the same.

Quantum physicists now say that every particle which is here can also exist in the farthest point of the universe at the same time. With this, separation can't exist. Being, which is here absolutely, is also there absolutely. There is no separation in this. In an absolute waking up, nothing happens. It is everywhere.

That's also why it is called *Ueber-all* (German word for "everywhere," which includes the word "all"). That which is Being is absolute, and it expresses or realizes itself absolutely in the nothing or in the all. But nothing realizes itself; it is still what it has always been. It never moved, which is why it is called a dreamlike movement. Nothing ever happens; nothing ever comes, nothing ever goes. There is never anything born that could die. Being is never born and will never die. No one can imagine this, but that's what you are.

Questioner
Can you repeat this again?

Karl
Being doesn't repeat itself.

He Perfers What is Within to What is Without

All paths are blindness.

Running and hunting make men's hearts crazy.
Rare goods make men's conduct confused.

Therefore, the Sage acts on what he feels
and not what he sees.
He prefers what is within to what is without.

If I said, "I will show you how you can find realization," it would be this blind man leading another blind man to something which leads to blindness. Because all paths are blind by nature. The absolute Seer is here and now, not sometime in the future, nor in the past, nor anywhere else.

A "path" is a useless tool which doesn't lead to that which you are, because you can't reach where you already are.

The path *is* the destination. This doesn't mean that the path will take you to the destination, or that the goal is to be on the path. No, very simply, "the path is the destination" means that you are *now already that* which you long for! And if you are not it *now*, then no path will ever lead you there.

You can only be it "here and now" because you can never be anywhere else at any other time.

The peace you long for is always just the reality that you are. And you will never know this reality; you can only *be* it absolutely. This you are, here and now. It will not happen on any path or through some kind of realization. The absolute realization that you don't have to understand anything *is* understanding. This is your nature.

There, nothing ever happens.

Welcome Disgrace Willingly

If, if, if . . .

Welcome disgrace willingly.
Accept it as a form of grace.
If you surrender yourself,
You will be steward of the world.

Questioner
I keep reading about the "dark night of the soul."

Karl
That's the last soul that falls.

Questioner
Does it have to be like this? It is always depicted so gruesomely that I feel outright horrified.

Karl
This is actually the most beautiful thing that can happen to you: a perfect depression. A total vacuum of meaning. A complete meaninglessness which overcomes you. This is what is called grace—it's the mercilessness in which you no longer see any meaning in the world, in spirit, or in anything. This is where the seeker is redeemed. But most of the time it doesn't end there, of course, but rather in some kind of pill-asylum. That's because there is still a running away from the meaninglessness or looking somewhere else for grace.

Everyone promises you heaven on earth, "If you only follow me." "If you do what I do"; if ... if ... if. "If you behave in a way that pleases God, then God will create paradise on earth for you"; if ... if ... if. "If I cross the dark night of the soul"; if ... if ... if. "There is another way, if you"; if ... if ... if.

This is what keeps the whole thing going.

One Looks For It And Doesn't See It

You are what you are.

One looks for it and doesn't see it
One listens for it and doesn't hear it
One grasps for it and doesn't feel it.
This is called the formless form,
the thing-less image.

The wish to know oneself is the most significant spiritual tendency one can have— precisely the wish that one's eternal happiness may be reached—the paradisiacal enlightenment where there is no one to be unhappy anymore.

At the beginning there is a basic tendency to move outward toward material bliss. Then, the idea of "I am" may occur and with it an inward tendency toward the bliss of oneness, the bliss of awareness. If it cannot find itself in all this, it may turn back toward itself—to being that, which is spirit, which is the Self, in order to find rest again.

Anything you can find cannot be that, which is your home. Thus, restlessness becomes your nature—even if you find nothingness—because even nothingness is a possession of someone who owns something.

The tendencies to search, to inquire, and to pray might be there, but they lead to nothing. Nothing comes out of it, thank God.

The fumbler continues to fumble, and if he can't cope with a particular teacher he just takes another. There will certainly be someone who tells you, "Do such-and-such to become freed from your egoic attachment of a "me." You'll feel better once you get rid of yourself, and so will the world."

How do you want to get rid of yourself? You are what you are!

This is what is so beautiful: that you are, before birth and after birth, only here and now. You never changed, nor can you *ever* change—even by desiring it, by seeking, by understanding, or even non-understanding.

Who Else Can Clear What Is Muddy Through Stillness?

Real seeing happens immediately.

Those who once were adept Masters,
were latently one with the unfathomable.
Deep they were, so one could not know them.
Who else can clear what is muddy
through stillness?

Each experience will happen when it happens. The experience of oneness or light will be there when it is there. It will not be rushed forth by your effort.

Nothing happens due to your effort or non-effort. The next moment is already existent in the absolute manifestation and it will not change whether you make an effort or not. Effort and effortlessness happen, unchangeably.

The stillness you can experience, or possibly need in order to be still, is just a conditional stillness. But your nature cannot be conditional on any circumstance, otherwise it wouldn't be your nature, as such.

Questioner
So it is impossible to reach it through reading, studying, working, or through stillness.

Karl

You can reach it—yourself—only by recognizing that
it cannot be reached through any way or method. For
that, it's worth every effort. Through that, it kills
itself. Only through the realization that you cannot
realize through "realization" can you realize.

This is the paradox: before you look into the light you
cannot say how it is. Only when you really *see* the light,
when you have the absolute experience that through
the experience of light your nature is neither increased
nor decreased, only then is it absolute reality.

This is not to be understood as an intellectual practice.
Real seeing, realizing, experiencing, happens immedi-
ately. It doesn't even happen. It just is. Immediately.
Obviously.

But if you just tell yourself intellectually, "Sure, I
can imagine that the light isn't it either," then there
always remains a doubt. The search then continues,
even if you think there is nothing to search for. It is
nothing but speculation.

Questioner

Why am I sitting here then?

Karl

Because this is exactly what totality ordered, but not
because there is someone who thinks he knows why he
is sitting here.

Question

I notice I just don't understand anything.

Karl

And that's what it is about. Whether you understand now or not doesn't make any difference to your nature.

16

Create Emptiness All The Way To The Highest!

Being needs absolutely no advantage.

Create emptiness all the way to the highest!
Keep to single-hearted stillness!
As all things rise and fall,
I contemplate their return.

Questioner

Who had the idea to separate himself from God?

Karl

God.

Questioner

OK, good, because we haven't found another one yet.

Karl

Do you mean "no other one?"

Questioner
Oh, never mind. It may be easier to determine that
there is no ego at all.

Karl
Only the ego determines this, because an ego is needed
to determine that there is no ego. Then, the ego thinks
it gained something because it now "knows" that there
is no ego.

It always requires one who thinks he has an advantage
from the ego's non-existence, and this one can only be
the ego. You just demonstrated this very well. You tried
to construct an advantage, and that's something only
an ego requires. Being needs absolutely no advantage.
When it comes to Being you can't create a necessity
for absence.

Questioner
So language can't express this at all.

Karl
Why not? The mind says, "I can't understand this,"
and by being able to it can remain as mind.

Questioner
Then only stillness remains.

Karl
Stillness for whom? Who needs this stillness?

Questioner
Nobody. Being doesn't need it. But people need the stillness.

Karl
What people?

Questioner
The ones who don't exist.

Karl
There you go—the lords of stillness. Stillness is controlled by its masters. Even worse than the heart-masters.

Questioner
With you one really can't talk.

Karl
Then just leave it.

When A Mighty One Rules

Being always knows how it needs be.

When a mighty one rules,
the people barely know that he is there.
Lesser ones are loved and praised,
other lesser ones are feared,
other lesser ones are despised.

I can only say: consciousness knows better than anyone else what there is to do, so it realizes again at some point to be consciousness.

Nobody here, who thinks that he exists, knows how it works. That includes my humble self. And this I find wonderful. Nobody knows it! It is a perfect mystery. Absolute consciousness always knows it absolutely better than anyone who thinks he knows it—including this thing here (Karl points to his body). This is wonderful to me. Absolute joy. No one can ever know it; no one can ever understand that there will never be a "second." That's because there has never been a first who could be understood. For me this is pure joy. Nothing brings this heart to shine, and to joy, as this!

Whenever and however you recognize this, it will never be the same way as anyone else. Everyone will have a unique experience. It will always be different, and it will always lead to the absence of separation between a subject and an object.

There are as many possibilities as there are humans in the world to find the way out of individuality. So there is no particular path, but for everyone it will be the right one. Being always knows how it needs to be.

No teacher can tell you how it needs to be, that it should be "such and such"—that's bullshit! This is why Jesus always points to the living word. Each so-called master points to the living word, not to dead books or dead stories. It is the living word that counts—where that which speaks, speaks to that which it is!

When The Tao Is Forgotten, There Arises Morality And Duty

In the Ashram one turns into ashes.

When the Tao is forgotten,
there arises morality and duty.
When cleverness and knowledge arise,
there appear big lies.

There is a book named *Fatelessness* (by Imre Kertész, winner of the Nobel Prize for literature. It's about life in the Buchenwald and Auschwitz concentration camps. Hydra Books, U.K.), which points directly to this: in the face of total tyranny, where one can be shot any moment, there exists periods of joy that are not caused by any circumstance. This is a clear pointer that joy or peace is not dependent on anything. Consciousness keeps creating circumstances for itself that are extreme enough for this "me" to break down.

The "me" lives from the past, because it thinks it has a future. But where no future is possible, the past also ends. You only need a past to cope with a future.

You want to learn from the past, so you calculate to figure out the future in order to arm yourself. But when there is no future for which you could or would have to arm yourself, the past stops. You don't need it.

Here, consciousness creates a concentration camp, which it focuses upon itself. This is an absolute inquiry—"Who am I?"

In India it's been said, "Hitler was an Avatar." Imagine that! In the end, it takes an avatar—who carries mercilessness within him—to send that many people into a concentration camp (or an ashram), where they turn into ashes. In that confrontation with death they have the possibility to experience their immortality.

Similarly, every ashram is a concentration camp where you grapple with your mortality, and question it in the face of death and the unavoidability of futurelessness. Is anything really "dying" in this so called death, when the body is gone?

These questions are a lot more relevant, direct, and burning, because there is the constant threat to our mortality. But what is mortal?

This is what is meant by "ashram," because one turns into ashes. One burns in the awareness of mortality, where you experience this bliss of the absolute *now*—the now that is "now and evermore" and not conditional. There is no focus on a relative hope for the future.

Dismiss Holiness, Throw Away Wisdom

This is the great joke that constantly takes place.

Dismiss holiness, throw away wisdom,
that way the people will benefit hundredfold.
See the simple and embrace the primal,
Let go of self.

The almighty God sits there amongst all his puppets. He's even turned into a puppet himself, adjusting himself to his puppets. Wonderful. And now, he even wants someone to liberate him from this. Poor guy! "His Grace"—grace itself—sits here and wants to be reprieved. This is the great joke that constantly takes place. Grace itself, which is the absolute Being, the absolute "I," the Self itself, sits in front of some apparent "other self" and expects that this assumed other self can teach him about his own nature.

This is why I call these talks "Self Talks," because things are not addressed that would require caring or some kind of attention; it is all just spontaneous.

Questioner
That's why you talk so fast.

Karl
Yes, I can't even follow myself. I love to listen to this because "I" could never say it. Even Jesus' statements

are only pointers to the unpronounceable.

The holy mountain, Arunachala, is also like a street sign, pointing "this is the way to the Self." You will not find yourself in the outer or the inner; you can never "find" yourself. That's just a pointer. And the beauty of this wonderful pointer is that you are not a relative object that can be found. So, you possibly find, in the absolute not-finding of your Self, that it was never lost.

20

I Have The Heart Of A Fool

Whether "homo" or "hetero,"
you remain ego-sexual.

I have the heart of a fool, confused and dark.
Worldly men are bright,
only I am muddy.
All men have their purposes;
only I am idle like a beggar.
But I consider it worth it,
to look for nourishment from the Mother.

The question "Who am I?" posed by Ramana Maharshi, points to the questioner who is also the answer. The absolute questioner is, at the same time, the answer to the question. And you are That, no matter whether your circumstance is oneness, two-ness, anything else, or whether this circumstance is accepted or rejected.

You are the absolute Self, and you know every trick there is to fool yourself into falling in love with yourself. You are such a charmer—the absolute charmer—so charming in your statements, so enticing in your expression, that you can keep bewitching yourself again and again.

You can't escape because you know yourself inside-out. You know exactly what is needed to fall for yourself, to fall for your own dream, again. You have no chance against yourself. You will always fail in not falling for yourself again.

You believe, "I have the tendency that one day I will no longer have any tendencies." The biggest trap! Again and again the expectation controls you that maybe, one day . . .

But everything that will come one day will also go again. Whether "homo" or "hetero," you remain ego-sexual.

The Content Of The Large Life Follows The Tao

The Self can't help itself.

The content of the large life
follows the Tao.
It is elusive and intangible,
and yet within is form.
How do I know the disposition of all things?
Precisely through them.

You already know everything. And you know that what you are doing right now would definitely not be good for you, if you existed. But you can't avoid it. This helplessness is the inherent characteristic of what you are—the helplessness of God or Being.

It is the nature of Being not to be able to help itself. The Self can't help itself since it would require a second. That which is energy has no energy with which it can "do" anything. Therefore, the source of ideas cannot know what flows out of it next.

You can't save yourself from yourself. This will-lessness or powerlessness is in itself paradise. This is what I call peace. There is no other who could dominate you, nor is there any other who you could dominate—including yourself. And you find no other whom you could dominate, not even yourself. That's the beauty of it.

As long as you—out of this powerlessness—want to have power or control, you suffer. Just think: what power do you have here? You are dependent on air to breathe, food to eat, and on the sun rising each day. You completely depend on your heart to beat and your lungs to breathe. If you don't get any air for five minutes, you won't exist any longer. What do you think you can control? You are constantly controlled by the body and by circumstance.

The *absolute* circumstance controls every aspect. You can't escape yourself; you can't go anywhere else. You will never be able to leave the here and now. You cannot *not* be yourself. You can't avoid any thought, any feeling, any insight, any experience, or any circumstance. Whatever happens or does not happen is inevitable.

This powerlessness is such sweetness in itself, which you can't taste because you *are* it. The sweetness is present because there is no need for sweetness.

What Is Partial Will Be Whole

The One can't be seen.

What is partial will be whole.
What is crooked will be straight.
What is empty will be full.

What is old will be new.
Who has little will receive.
Who has plenty will be confused.

The idea that there is a second, that there are others,
is born out of the idea that there is a first. And because the first cannot exist without a second, it simply
imagines a second. It would be boring otherwise, and
impossible, too. This is where the crisis already starts:
something second is needed—something different
from the first—so you create a playmate for yourself,
but it is never enough. The game is never enough!

As soon as the subtlest "I" of awareness arises it asks
itself "I-am what?"; "I-am what?" Immediately the
answer occurs, "The world."

Suddenly all the answers are there, but you can always
see just one aspect of it. You only get one tiny partial
answer, with which you are not satisfied. You can
never be satisfied with partial aspects, because there
is always something missing—no matter how good the
deception is, no matter how wonderfully deceived you
are, no matter how you appear to yourself.

You can never see the whole, because the whole is not
visible. Otherwise, you would have to see yourself, and
seeing or perceiving doesn't work without a second.
The One, the whole, cannot be *seen*.

At most, you can return to that which you are. Then
there are no more parts, nor connections, nor anything.
You simply are. You are all parts, all connections, all

separations, in all places, at all times, and in all beings. In this *allness*, any kind of "isness" is impossible. You can never be anything other than yourself. You can never perceive anything else again, and you can't even perceive yourself. There are no more possibilities.

Thus, you are everything and nothing.

Make Rare The Words, Then Everything Happens By Itself

Consciousness experiences a never-ending self-exploration.

Make rare the words,
then everything happens by itself.
A tornado doesn't last for a morning.
A downpour doesn't last for a day.
And who causes these?
Heaven and earth.
If Heaven and earth
can't make these eternal,
then how much less so can man?

You should know yourself the way you are in deep sleep, because in deep sleep you exist without the "knower" or an object to be known.

Know yourself as what you are, despite everything
that the experiencer can or cannot experience.

You are the experiencer, but this is not a "somebody"
or a "something." You *are*. This you can't even know,
you can only *be* it.

It doesn't mean that you should always be in deep
sleep. That's not possible. What happens, happens.
Whether you want it or not. You are you, here and now,
always as you are right now. More is not more and less
is not less. More is not even possible. However, for the
hungry "me" ghost it will never be enough.

Consciousness, which is me, will always look for itself.
Consciousness experiences a never-ending self-exploration—the eternal search for that, which it is. When
you realize that this will never end, it ends. That's the
wonderful paradox.

The expectation that it will happen at a certain point
falls away. And in the falling away of "the expectation
that something may fall away," the *expecter* also falls
away.

Everything still takes place, nevertheless. The exact
same things have happened since time immemorial.
Nothing changes. The realization of exit-lessness happens, when it happens. And if not, then not. You can't
do anything about it. Nothing at all.

In all this there is no "mine" that you can recognize
here and now. The whole is conditional unto itself, in

all its aspects. Do you feel how peaceful this is? When all your acting and doing doesn't help, you might as well leave it—but it's only then, when you can. You can only leave it, when you leave it. And if you don't leave it, you have no chance of leaving it. Is this not wonderful?

He Who Stands On Tiptoes, Does Not Stand Firm

You cannot want what you want.

He who stands on tiptoes,
does not stand firm.
He who walks with splayed legs,
does not advance.
He who wants to shine himself,
will not get enlightened.

Questioner
So I can do whatever I want?

Karl
You can only do what you want if you could "want" what you want—but you cannot want what you want.

With this, every idea of willful acting drops. It is the absence of an idea of free will. Even when you decide, you cannot decide what you decide, because the decision is already made. You still experience "decision," yet there is no one, through the experience of free will, who has it. The experience of free will just happens.

This is the essence: "free will" "no free will." These are two different forms of perception and nothing else. It always takes one who perceives differently, and that one is an experience already.

But you are—uninterruptedly—what you are, which is also here and now. You are that which you are, despite the relative experience of will and no-will.

25

The Tao Follows Itself

You are the will but you don't "have" any.

Four mighty ones there are in the universe,
and man is also amongst
them.
Man follows the earth.
The earth follows Heaven.
Heaven follows the Tao.
The Tao follows itself.

You are the will, but you don't "have" any. You are power but you don't "have" any. You are energy but you don't "have" any. You are consciousness but you don't "have" any.

You possess nothing that could do anything. You are happening, and you happened. You are history, but you don't "have" any history.

And you, who have no consciousness, also have no idea if something is bigger or smaller. There is no quantity of consciousness. Everything that thinks it has a consciousness certainly doesn't have any. It has all kinds of things, but no consciousness.

Consciousness does not own or know itself, since there are not two. This is everybody's quality and nature. The consciousness that can be "known" or one can be "aware of" is merely an idea. Bigger or smaller, more aware or less aware—all belong to the world of phantoms.

You are completely uncontrollable, without any control. You are God and you are the powerlessness of God. And the beautiful thing is: it doesn't matter.

The Omnipotence can want everything, but it cannot "want" what it wants. If it could want what it wants, then it would already have to want the "wanting what it wants." Then you would have to find the beginning of wanting, and there would have to have been a big bang, thus an original wanting. Then there would be a beginning of awareness.

The potential Being, which knows neither awakeness nor non-awakeness, can neither want nor be awake.

This spontaneous imagining of awakeness is an involuntary awakening, but not because it wants to awaken.

Stillness Is The Ruler Of Restlessness

Only in two-ness there is suffering.

The heavy is the root of the light.
Stillness is the ruler of restlessness.

Therefore, though the Sage has
magnificence in front of his eyes,
He rests serenely in his solitude.

Questioner
So this is a nice excuse, that Being wanted it this way?

Karl
Yes, one could say that, too. One can always fiddle it the way one wants to: "If Being wants it, then I will just suffer from myself; there is no way out."

Only in two-ness there is suffering. And this is always an illusion in itself, a deception. It is only possible for something to suffer under something else. The

Almighty happens to be so almighty in his perception, in his attention, that he can even, when he falls in love with an imagination, suffer from his own imagination. So he always suffers from himself, even if it is only an imagination.

The freedom from suffering is the absence of a sufferer.

You can see that anything possible, such as having children—and whatever else you do or don't do—points towards bliss. But only through no action, or no wish, or no manifestation will you reach what you long for. Only in this stillness, this complete resignation in relation to everything, can the absolute resignation—in which the resigner is shaved off—happen through Grace, which doesn't even know Grace. This falls when it falls, and not when you want, because the "wanting" to fall is in opposition to this.

A Good Traveler Doesn't Leave Tracks

You listen eternally to that which you are.

A good traveler doesn't leave tracks.
A good speaker doesn't need to disprove anything.

Questioner
Why don't you tell us why we are sitting here?

Karl
Because the Self never gets enough of listening to
what the Self is or is not. This has no beginning and
no end. You listen eternally to that which you are. In
this instant, when you listen here, you possibly listen
to the listener. Perhaps the listener will move into
awareness, because he is always being addressed here.
Here, no relative person is addressed, because for me
there is no personal progress. That which is addressed
here is already now, absolute, and is what it is, without
any limitations.

Your nature does not depend on clarity. Since it is not
dependent, clarity is joy. If you were dependent on
clarity, this would be a damn prison.

Because you don't get clearer through clarity—or
less clear through non-clarity—both are joy. This is
the uninterrupted joy of that which you are. Not dependent on a clear one ("clear one" in German also
means *schnaps* or whiskey), then another clear one,
then another clear one is the self-drunkenness that
you cannot create through any drink, nor any
meditation nor any knowledge. This self-
drunkenness, this joy, is not
dependent on anything.
This peace is a joy that cannot be described. It is the total
gratefulness, the absolute gratefulness, in which you don't have to thank

anyone in order to be what you are—no God, no master, no teacher, no guru, no one, nothing.

This absolute joy doesn't require joy to *be* joy. You never get enough.

Questioner
And somehow one gets addicted.

Karl
Absolutely self-addicted. You are that, anyway, you don't need to become that.

Whoever Knows His Purity

Passion gets paid for with pain.

Whoever knows his purity
and keeps his weakness,
is an example to the world.
If he is an example to the world,
eternal life won't leave him,
and he returns again to the Unborn.

You had so much desire to live that you came out of this—with desire it starts—the desire to know yourself. Out of this sheer desire, this whole circus came about. And out of this desire, out of this primordial

urge to wake up, to want to know oneself, this first
desire for yourself, the whole lust-palace emerged.

No chance. This divine comedy/tragedy, this passion to
know oneself, happens by desire, and passion gets paid
for with pain.

Any attempt to want to know oneself is in itself painful
and everything you experience is a result of that. Out
of this divine accident, you began by wanting to know
yourself and you woke up. Even God couldn't help it.
That is why it is called an "accident." He couldn't even
decide beforehand that he would wake up. Because
before waking up there is no one to decide whether
he wants to wake up. Thus, a spontaneous awakening
just happens.

Really, with the initial idea that you exist, the first
drama begins. You can't escape this! It keeps happening over and over. No matter how you understood it,
or what you believe you have realized, how deeply you
penetrated your Being, how tolerantly you were born,
you will always be fooled by yourself again. It can't be
helped.

The World Is A Spiritual Thing

Everything is *always.*

The world is a spiritual thing
that cannot be improved.
The one who tampers with it, damages it,
the one who wants to grasp it, loses it.

Everything is being dreamt, even the dream that you
are able to decide anything. In this moment, the past,
the future, and the present already exist in their po-
tentiality. Everything *is* always. Being is never-never.

Reality and realization are not different. Being knows
no coming or going. "Nothing ever happened" is a
pointer that nothing was ever born and nothing will
ever die. The next moment is already here; it will neither come nor will it go.

Nietzsche spoke of the "Eternal return of the same"
and said, "Recognize eternity as a moment which
keeps repeating itself infinitely." With this, your hope
for a future becomes superfluous. You will always be
back here again, as stupid as today.

Everything that apparently happens has already happened. Therefore, nothing ever realized itself. Reality
and realization are unmovable. There is absolutely no
possibility of change; everything is absolute in itself.

The One Who Follows
The Laws Of The Universe

There is no other player.

The one who follows the laws of the universe
doesn't seek to control the world by violence;
because he knows, everything rebounds upon himself.

Being has these two basic tendencies: one is the struggle
for survival of the body, the person. The other is grace,
the longing to return. Both are inexhaustible, both
come out of the same source. There is the tendency to
preserve oneself, and the tendency to disappear, and
both tendencies fight with each other. Sometimes one
wins, sometimes the other. For Being it is absolutely
irrelevant who wins; it is playing with itself after all.
There is no other player.

To wait for this to stop at some point and to end in
peace is hopeless. Nothing can make you into that
which you already are. In both tendencies you are
what you are, because you are the *source* of both. Both,
in themselves, are as infinite as you are!

The expectation that anything will win can last forever. It is precisely this expectation—that you will "find
yourself," through one or the other tendency—that
lets you be a relative object that depends upon winning
or losing.

It can change—something can always change—but it will absolutely not change that which you are.

Weapons Are Instruments of Fear

The idea of love discriminates against hatred.

Weapons are instruments of fear;
all beings hate them.
Therefore the wise
avoid them.

Questioner
There is love, but hatred is a disturbing feeling.

Karl
The opinion "I can accept love, but not hatred" is fascism. It is the nature of fascism to discriminate, and the idea of love discriminates against hatred. For this it takes a discriminator—that's the fascist.

In the name of love so much shit has already happened. In the name of freedom, in the name of truth, in the name of God, too. It can't get any worse.

Then we have the ones with the open hearts—they are the little hearts who beat up others who they believe still have closed hearts. This is really the worst fascist

way—running around making others feel guilty because they still have closed hearts. The heart-masters.

The Eternal Tao Is Nameless Innocence

There is no before and no after.

The eternal Tao is nameless innocence.
When creating starts, only then are there names.

You can't escape that which you are, and this I call
peace. For peace, nothing continues, there is no next
moment or anything further. There is no before and no
after—never has been.

And you won't be able to cope with this. But it can
cope with you. If you are after Grace you won't find
it, for sure. But if Grace is after you, then "God have
mercy!" But it never hits anyone, that's the beauty.

We see this in the example of Ramana Maharshi,
because he was often asked, "Ramana, what is your
realization? Are you a realized one?" Ramana would
often point out: that, which is seen as Ramana, can't
realize anything; that, which *is* Ramana is eternally
realized and doesn't need to *become* realized.

So, your nature is already here and now. It doesn't

need to be made real. And that, which is an "aspect" of realization, is unable to be made real, either. Is this not magnificent!

The One Who Knows Himself Is Wise

There is simply an "Aha."

He who knows others is smart.
He who knows himself is wise.
He who doesn't perish in death is eternal.

Questioner
Can one say that avatars reincarnate?

Karl
That's their nature, it's part of the dream.

Questioner
The Sat-Guru doesn't return?

Karl
He was never here. If the Dalai Lama stopped the wheel of reincarnation, that would be it: the absolute realization that his birth never happened, that he is "that which was never born." Then, the absolute stopping of the wheel of reincarnation would take place. But an avatar, who goes from one life to the next, is

still stuck in the wheel of reincarnation no matter how high he rises. He may reach the highest level of reincarnation, but he will still be reborn again. There is still someone who turns into one thing from another. Even this is still an illusion, still a dream—all part of the entertainment. And, if Being arranges it like this, why not?

To think that this could be seen as an advantage, that one could control it when one comes back, is still a form of suffering. Buddha always pointed this out. The idea that you exist at all, is suffering itself.

There is this absolute resignation: Haunted by the longing to improve or change yourself, you finally really see that there is no way out of that which you are, neither now nor later.

You can never become that what you already are! Nothing "happens," there is simply an "Aha"—a seeing that what you are, you have always been and always will be. What you are is outside of time. Time exists because of you; it simply reflects that which you are.

Don't make an event out of it. It is not a happening. You simply see "that which you are" is the only reality, and that it is never touched by any perception. This is nothing new, it is ancient and infinite. You only see, "Aha, oh, infinity"—everything that exists is the infinite, and this is neither an experience nor a happening.

The Tao Flows Everywhere

This is the preservation of the Dharma.

The Tao flows everywhere,
both to the right and to the left.
All things owe their existence to it,
and it doesn't deny itself to them.

Questioner
What is the deal about the ideas of purity,
such as, "to lead a pure life" and "to strive
for kindness, like a Bodhisattva?"

Karl
This is the preservation of the Dharma. It keeps the
teaching, which is an idea, alive.

Questioner
Is there an advantage to be good?

Karl
As long as you want to be good, it is an advantage to be
good. And as long as you believe that being good makes
you happy, it is better for you to be good.

Questioner
But it drives some people crazy to be bad.

Karl

Yes, in the same way as being good. Both come from the ignorant idea that one needs something other than that which one is in order to be complete or happy. Just see that what you are *is* complete, and that ideas of imperfection are just ideas that can't touch perfection, as such.

The World Will Come To Him, Who Holds On To The One

Don't follow any examples.

The world will come To him,
who holds on to the One.
It comes and will not be hurt;
For there lies rest, equanimity, and beatitude.

You want to find your own question? First try to find out what you are. Then, I can promise you, there will be stillness. There is no question that it belongs to you. You will never find your own question. There is simply just peace. There is no questioner; the questioner is a mix of questions, of conditioning, that's all.

One reads a lot of books from whomever—fairy tale hour, nothing else. These are not your questions. Your basic question is always directed to self-realization.

Don't follow any examples; there are neither good nor bad examples for finding yourself. You won't find your-self through any masters; you will only find yourself in the absolute confrontation with the seer, which you are. And not as a questioner who asked something at a certain point. You can, here and now, look at what looks at itself. You can be what the absolute seer is: that which can never be found, and devoid of any con-cept of a person.

There is nothing except that which you are. There are no other Gods without you. There will never be a God who can help you out of this. There is no one who can console you, and this desolation is peace and joy.

Do you know what depression means? Depression is the absolute vacuum of a second. There only remains what you are—without a second. You haven't expe-rienced this yet because there is "no one" who could come out of it.

But what you call depression is more like the feeling, "I don't feel well; I feel lousy." Where there is a vacuum, there is a total absence of pressure. There, you don't feel bad, you don't feel at all.

The Soft Overcomes The Hard

I am even pulling out the flying carpet.

If you want to take,
you first have to give fully.
This means clarity over the invisible.
The soft overcomes the hard
The weak defeats the strong.

Identification is an infection. You have a virus: it's the idea that you exist as this body, which is separate from the rest. This is the infection. It's a kind of disease, against which nothing helps. But the sick one wants to get well, and by wanting to get well he makes a disease out of health.

I am everything, I was everything. I have done everything already; I don't even have to think of it in this moment. Even the "moment" I made. I am *prior* to and beyond any kind of imagination.

It is a kind of realization that there is no "experience," that any experience is the opposite of something else.

I am in every way absolute, I am everywhere. No matter which way you turn, I am there. No escape. If you sit in front of anyone, you always sit in front of *me*, thus, in front of *yourself*.

You can't escape *me*, I am always and everywhere. You can take it any way you want, because there is *absolutely* someone there, yet there is no one there. Thus, I teach emptiness. I am a rug puller; I am even pulling out the flying carpet.

Before his death, Nisargadatta Maharaj is supposed to have said, "Now this body, which is called 'Nisargadatta,' leaves me and still no one cares what the body did or did not do." This is the most present one can be. So, let it get you, succumb to the war.

The Tao Is Eternally Without Doing

There is no one who ever realized anything.

The Tao is eternally without doing
and nothing remains undone.

Desirelessness produces stillness,
and the world becomes settled by itself.

You are both reality and the realization. You can't separate them. Just look at the words "real" and "realization" next to each other! It is the real and also the unfolding of the real within time and space.

Is there ever a moment in time when you are not realized? On the other hand, that which you now take yourself to be will never be realized. How could an idea become realized? It is not true.

Realization means that consciousness, which once was identified with an object, becomes boundary-less. It becomes conscious of being consciousness. But the Self is never realized nor not-realized. It is always prior to any ideas about enlightenment and non-enlighten-ment, no matter what you say about it. Anything you can say about it is an idea.

There is no one who ever realized anything—not even Karl who is part of this realization.

He Who Upholds Life

*Know yourself the way you know
yourself in deep sleep!*

He who upholds life,
doesn't know anything about life;
that's why he has life.

He who doesn't uphold life,
seeks not to lose life;
that's why he has no life.

Questioner
Would you say that you are an awakened one?

Karl
I would never say this. But I would also never say, "I am not." I have no idea.

Questioner
One can actually not know it.

Karl
One can know it, but it wouldn't interest anyone.

Questioner
Not even yourself?

Karl
It wouldn't interest me whether it interests me. So, I wouldn't care if I cared or didn't care about it. Because this is caretaker-freedom.

Questioner
Can you recognize that you are awakened?

Karl
Where there is an awakened one, there is still the ignorance of a lunatic who thinks that he once slept. Everything that has a "before" or "after" happens in the dream.

Every night, in deep sleep, you have the direct experience—that there is neither one born nor one unborn.

Both are ideas. To be one who is unborn is already an idea.

For the idea of being born and not being born to emerge at all, there first has to be that which you are—that, which is prior to imagination.

You are that every night in deep sleep. No one has to teach you this. The absence of a perceiver and something perceivable is your natural state.

Know yourself the way you know yourself in deep sleep! And this is to be poor in spirit. It's the absolute poverty—to not even possess an idea of what you are or are not. This is unconditional Being.

All Is Created By The One

Consciousness dances.

All is created by the One.
If heaven were not thus pure,
it would have to burst.
If the earth were not thus firm,
it would have to tremble.
If all things were not created by this,
they would have to be extinguished.

Peace doesn't come and doesn't go. More peace is not possible. Only one thing always causes trouble—that you think you have to make it into *your* peace, and it should be as you imagine that peace to be. Then it becomes a problem. Then you become Mr. Bush, which means you have to go to Iraq and create peace there, too. Because there are six and one-half billion ideas of how peace, or how the world should be, there are so many wars. My goodness! Everything because of peace or the idea of it.

Consciousness dances, gee, but nothing happens.

Questioner
But is not what Mr. Bush did in Iraq also part of consciousness?

Karl
Absolutely. It is an absolute aspect of realization. And if this aspect of realization—"Bush in Iraq"—didn't exist, the whole of Being wouldn't exist. Because the absoluteness of Being has to express itself in all possible and impossible aspects. One aspect of this is "Mr. Bush who wages war."

In each tiniest action the absolute is contained. If you could prevent even one thing, you could prevent yourself.

Questioner
So Bush is also not responsible for it?

Karl
Bush as "Bush" doesn't exist at all. Really recognize, here and now, that there never has been any action that you did that is yours, and that there is no owner of Being. Then, this poor little me just makes a pling [!] in the realization that Being can't be owned. And without Being—being what it is—nothing could be. That's peace.

Being Is Born Out Of Non-Being

It doesn't matter how deep you penetrate,
you will never arrive where you already are.

Returning is the motion of the Tao.
Yielding is the way of the Tao.
All things under the sky come out of Being.
Being is born out of Non-Being.

"Fictitious" is a word you have to see properly. The German word for "fictitious" is *fiktiv*, which sounds like *fick tief* or "fuck deep." This means that it doesn't matter how deep you penetrate, you will never arrive where you already are.

Ficken is an old German word that was used in the past to describe the process in which a sword is inserted and pulled out of white heat. This way, the iron was hardened and sharpened. This was called *ficken*.

Always sharp. *Engelhardt* is, "the heart of the angel," where the embers are hottest.

And this is also awareness—the purest light where the heat is strongest. And here is precisely in and out—*Fiktiv*. Man, this is some language! You take this into your mouth every day and think you are not sexual all the time? This is total sexuality here and now. It's the expectation that through some experience you could finally "come" absolutely, so you would then finally be "gone" absolutely—it's the avoidance of self, no matter which way that you try!

The Great Tone Has Inaudible Sound

Animals are closer to meditating.

The great tone has inaudible sound.
The great image has no form.
The Tao in its mysteriousness is without name.

Sometimes you focus on the world, another time on yourself. Both are not different. You get out of it anyway, you escape what you are. You orient yourself, once in a while, toward that which is *prior* to everything, and then to that which is the realization of it. In both cases you are what you are. It will never get better. This is called peace.

Questioner
What distinguishes us from animals in this way? The
cat is wide awake yet it doesn't bother with our philosophy.

Karl
Yes, and that's why one meditates, The German word
for "meditation" is *mediTIERen*, which contains the
word *tier* (animal)—that's because animals are closer
to this. How do you actually meditate properly? Just
show me. Does one sit down and makes the proper
facial expression, imagine light, the final awareness,
meditates on *Om*, or all of these techniques? How do
you do it? Do you have the power to do it? Does it matter? It is fun.

What's wonderful about all this meditation is that,
thank God, nothing comes out of it. That would really
be the worst thing of all, if through the tactic of an
exercise, that which you are—your essence—could be
reached. But the illusion that this could happen keeps
the whole thing going.

The Tao Creates The One

The trinity, which is three, is equal to one.

The Tao creates the one.
The one creates the two.

The two creates the three.
The three creates all things.
All things have their back to the dark
and strive for the light,
and the blending of these gives them harmony.

The trinity—awareness, consciousness, known—is one. Not three "aspects" of one, but one, without difference. So the trinity, which is three, is equal to one. Deep sleep is awareness, which is why I also call that which is awareness, "deep-deep sleep."

This is not the presence of absence; it is the absence of presence. It is the absence of the presence of the one who could or could not be aware.

That, which you are, is the nature of Nisargadatta, Jesus, and so on. You don't have to envy them. You don't have to become like them, nor do you have to refuse what they reveal. They are what you are: the absolute seer and the absolute perception.

The truth, which becomes a perceiver, perceives, and is perceived as something, is absolutely indistinguishable from itself. It's not separable; you can't separate yourself from yourself, nor can you separate anything from you. You are spaceless, timeless, yet separation is impossible. You have no mass and no energy. You are all that, but you don't "possess" it.

The nature of Nisargadatta and your nature are not different. Whether you stay in awareness and perceive in deep sleep, or if you are in the consciousness of experience in deep-deep sleep, is totally irrelevant for your nature. You won't become more or less through any of these circumstances.

It doesn't matter if you experience yourself in the relative or in Oneness, whether in daily consciousness or in the "I Am," or even in the Awareness-"I," in the so-called *Atman*, or Light-Consciousness. In all these three possibilities you realize yourself, but through none of these realizations you become more real.

Your reality won't be increased or decreased through any of the ways in which you experience yourself.

Teaching Without Words

Just see!

That which has no substance penetrates
even the densest of things.
That's how one recognizes the value of non-acting.
The teaching without words, the value of non-doing,
only few on earth attain.

One idea of mankind is: "I am conscious; one of my characteristics is consciousness." This happens based on the sensation of separation. We experience ourselves as a separate person.

Consciousness plays the role of the person, but there is no person who "owns" consciousness. If there is any possession at all, then it is that of consciousness, which owns the person.

The only thing that is not conceptual is the Self. With the help of concepts you can look at things from infinite perspectives and keep inventing new and different concepts. But this doesn't need an explanation!

This is only about seeing—to point to the core—to see that only the Self is reality.

And this reality is *prior* to all ideas about existence or non-existence. Each idea that shows up is fiction. That which is prior to fiction, prior to ideas, is that which you are.

To replace one concept with another concept in order to get a "clear concept," doesn't bring any advantage. This has nothing to do with understanding. Seriously, it has nothing to do; it does nothing. It doesn't even bite. Just see!

The Self is all, and whatever happens, only happens within and through the Self.

Winning Or Losing: Which Is Worse?

There will never be a saucer
that can realize Being.

The name or the person:
which matters more?
The person or the possession:
which is more precious?
Winning or losing:
which is worse?

Questioner

There are people who believe that an evolution is taking place.

Karl

Yes, that exists too, but namely for this "me"-ghost, which is constantly trying to confirm itself by creating something incomprehensible, then doing exercises and practicing again and again. It's never ending. In this way it keeps confirming, "I can't achieve it; I want it all; I want to realize. I want to be the first realized one who ever entered the world. Me! Why not me? There was, after all, a Ramana, a Mohammed, a Buddha, and all the other realized ones. Why them, why not me?"

All this, even though the so-called realized ones have said that there never was a realized one.

In the same way, there will never be a saucer that can realize Being. But "you," nevertheless, keep trying to create the impossible so that you will be the first—and only one—who ever realized what Being is.

Great Fullness Seems Empty

The Self does not depend on anything.

Great perfection seems imperfect,
yet it becomes infinite in its effect.
Great fullness seems empty,
yet it cannot be exhausted.
Purity and stillness are the world's measure.

When you see that nothing ever happened, there are no more steps. You are what you always have been and always will be. The rest is simply a theater play. The Self does not depend on anything. Whether you see the Self as source of everything, or not, is of no use whatsoever for the Self since it neither recognizes nor ignores anything. To become clear about something at some particular point is meaningless; you are clarity itself.

The first unfolding is awareness; it is a sense of the Self, which is aware of existence. So there is the Self, which is aware of its separation. Awareness is *already* separation; it functions, but is not "that which func-

tions." One can call it the source of the "I am," which
is the source of "I am Karl."

In the same way that the eye can't see itself, the absolute definer can't define what the definer is. What you
are cannot avoid resting in itself, nor can it not rest in
anything else, because the Self is all there is.

You can't escape it because you are the Self. Wherever
you go, nobody moves and nobody stands still. Just see
the totality of that which you are, even in the world
of time and space. The totality is all there is. Even
this image, which calls itself "I," which pops up in the
morning and disappears again in the evening, doesn't
need realization.

As long as you believe that you are this image, as long
as the "I"-thought is your reality, then the Self is only
an idea. It is consciousness that is looking for itself.

As long as you take yourself for a person who is trapped
in time, there will always be difficulties. There is no
way out, and there doesn't need to be one.

There is no end of suffering. Look for the "beginning";
if you find the beginning then you may be in the po-
sition to find the end of suffering. Did suffering ever
begin? For suffering to be present, there needs to be
a sufferer, so look first for the sufferer. As long as you
are looking for the end of suffering, the sufferer will
continue to exist.

The sense of "I am" does bring a sufferer with it.

Therefore, the only way is to extinguish the sufferer. When the sufferer is extinguished, where is there suffering?

To Be Content With Contentment Is Permanent Contentment

Who cares about an appearance?

When the Tao rules on earth,
the race horses are drawn to pull dung.
When the Tao is absent from earth,
war horses are bred in the meadow.

There is no bigger mistake then wanting to have.
Therefore, to be content with
contentment is permanent contentment.

Questioner
What is the difference between the seeker who listens to talks like this, for so many years now, and the butcher who is not interested in this subject but who wants to make a lot of money, have a nice house, and just be happy?

Karl
Good steaks and good Schnitzel.

Both want to be happy, absolutely happy. Due to the ignorance about what they already are, they strive for absolute happiness. The idea of separation incudes a sense of imperfection, which drives both of them to look for perfection—not knowing that they are the absolute perfection. This is why the butcher and the seeker are consciousness that is looking for satisfaction. There is no difference between them.

Questioner
So it doesn't help to listen to you again and again over a period of several years? What advice would you give to the earnest seeker who dedicates his or her life to the striving for enlightenment?

Karl
Imagine if there is someone who could be helped and someone who could give that help. That would be hell. Don't listen to anyone, not even to yourself. Whatever you perceive cannot be you. Everything you've understood you can forget again. The belief in a being, who could become clear about something, is not what you are.

Questioner
But there is the opinion that the ego is slowly and gradually becomes less.

Karl
Less ego, more ego. What can disappear can also emerge again. The ego that disappears may return sooner or later. Look first what really appears and whether this apparition is real. Because: who cares about an appear-

ance? This is the most important question that should be asked; not the question about what comes and goes.

How absurd, to care about an apparition. The belief in a separate self, who takes an apparition for real, is pure ignorance.

Without Looking Out Of The Window, One Sees The Tao Of Heaven

Satsang is no higher experience than a sip of coffee.

Without looking out of the window,
one sees the Tao of Heaven.

The farther one goes out,
the less one's knowledge becomes.

All realizations are fleeting, thank God. No matter how deep they are, how magnificent they sound, and how enlightening they appear. They are actually just nonsense. Each sip of coffee is as equal to the realization of Being as the biggest world-realization of your deepest soul-quality. You can only experience yourself, and you experience that in both the smallest and biggest tastes. Anything you can taste is an aspect of your nature, but you will never be able to taste the "taster." The taster that you can taste is an object to be tasted, but not that, which the taster is. Did you taste that now?

Questioner
Are energetic phenomena, which one experiences in a satsang, also illusionary?

Karl
Of course. Equally illusionary as the just mentioned sip of coffee.

Questioner
But also equally enjoyable?

Karl
Equally. Value is a stamp. A definition. A make-up. An illusion. Satsang is no higher an experience than sipping a cup of coffee. A sip of coffee has the same value of self-experience as any kind of satsang, any *shakti*, or any other experience of energy. Even if you experienced the sun, it would still be a self-experience that wouldn't be worth more than the sip of coffee.

Consciousness is the most stupid thing you can imagine. It always adjusts to the circumstance it finds itself in. Even worse, it is simply the circumstance that it experiences. The quality is always the one and only— it's the Self that experiences itself.

In Non-Doing, Nothing Is Left Undone

I can turn it whichever way I want;
nothing will come out of it!

Whoever practices learning, adds something daily,
Whoever practices the Tao, drops something daily.
He drops and drops,
until he finally arrives at non-doing.
In non-doing, nothing is left undone.

I am constantly talking about irrelevance, and that there is no one who could get anything here. There is no one at all who could give anything to another, yet someone sits in front of me who says exactly the opposite. This means that, for the past five years, I've actually talked for nothing.

Thank God! I am happy that even this was for nothing. I am happy that I even failed in failing, especially when I told everyone "you can only fail," and that you then say you didn't fail. This is really a *Scheiterhaufen* (word play on the German word for "funeral pile," which includes the German word "to fail").

So everything I say is totally pointless. But it is pure joy. If I were happy that someone does not return here, it would mean that there is someone who could have left. That would really be terrible. I can turn it whichever way I want; nothing will come out of it!

Ramana called this, "good company." Good company also means "no company"—when one leaves his companions behind.

The Sage Lives In The World Totally Still

Heart is the essence.

The Sage does not have a heart of his own.
He makes the heart of the people his heart.

The Sage lives in the world totally still
and opens his heart wide for the world.

David Bowie was asked, "What is the difference between esoterics and spiritual seekers?" He said, "Esoterics want to be in heaven, and spiritual seekers went through hell." Hell . . . that's Shiva. As soon as you believe you made it, Shiva will show *you* who made it. Then, he'll really chop away at you.

Questioner
Yes, that one I already know!

Karl
You didn't get to know Shiva properly; otherwise you wouldn't speak of love anymore. Because love really

stops there. Shiva destroys the last glimmer you have, any hope you have, and any idea you have about how love should or should not be.

He beats all that back into its original ground, but not the way you imagine. It takes you away. This is the love that mercilessly lets everything, which isn't grace, drop. It becomes merciless towards mercy. This is the mercilessness of existence, and what you call Shiva, or love, has no love in it or outside of it.

There is nothing else but heart. Every thought, every idea, wanting or not-wanting, comes straight from the heart. The original ground of thought is the original ground of the thinker: that which is heart. Without heart there is no one who could have any ideas. Intuition comes directly from the heart, but the heart is not an intuition. Heart is the *essence*—your Self—the essence of Being.

Coming Out Of Non-Beingness Into Beingness Is Birth

The eternal life is reality and *its realization.*

Coming out of non-beingness into beingness is birth; returning back to non-beingness is death.

There is a famous story of Lord Rama, who goes to a
saint and is taught *Advaita*—that you are not the body,
you are not this, not that, etc. Lord Rama realizes that
he is not the body, not the spirit, and not awareness.
He is "That."

Full of gratitude for this realization, Rama wants to
give the saint his diamond ring. The sage takes the
ring, opens a basket full of diamond rings, and throws
Rama's diamond ring into it, saying "See you next
time!"

Therefore, this moment has already occurred to you
infinite times. Everything that you realize you will
have to realize over and over again. But reality, which
is always there, will not become more real than it already is through realization.

Nature is in itself unborn Being. Something that is
never born can never be changed, nor will it ever die.
The eternal life is that which is. The eternal life is
reality *and* its realization—there is no difference. Any
question of predestination is irrelevant here.

There is only the hopelessness of no escape of that
which you are. You can't escape this, and for this you
need to do absolutely nothing.

One can only be that, which is light, but one can't possess light. All striving comes from the idea of ownership. Just recognize that the owner can never "own"
enlightenment. That you can never be "owned," nor
belong to anything or anyone, is pure joy. The idea of

knowledge is already hell, so I am an ambassador of joy. Let the idea of an owner drop and nothing is there.

51

The Tao Creates

You have no choice.

The Tao creates.
Life nourishes.
The environment forms.
The influences complete.

The moment you experience yourself as born, you are in an existential crisis. Now you have to manage that crisis, which is normal. Just that the idea that you were "born" is insanity.

Out of this insane holding on, to being someone who was born, all of the other insanities immediately emerge—such as the destitution and longing to return to freedom, to that bliss, which is your nature.

There is "no one" who is this, nor no one who is not it. Bliss is the absence of an idea of existence or non-existence. But the moment the idea of existence becomes real for you, there is also non-existence—the opposite. In this moment you are stuck in duality and become afraid of non-existence, of mortality.

I am describing a process that has to be the way it is. You can recognize "that which happens" as a process, but it doesn't mean anything for that which you are. This is because you are *prior* to the concept of process, fear, and a fearer. The only thing that you know is "you are."

You have no choice. When you speak, you speak; when you are silent, you are silent. Not because you want to. You can't even escape any kind of stupidity; stupidities are made to be committed.

To Choose The Soft, Means Being Strong

There is no second, there is nothing but This.

To see the smallest, means to see clearly.
To choose the soft, means being strong.
If one uses one's light
to get back to this clarity,
then one doesn't endanger oneself.
This is called the shell of eternity.

Jesus went into the totality—into not-knowing—into the absence of experience, and then he was reborn into pure absolute awareness. He was just "this." It is that which is light, that which is consciousness, that which is space, and that which is the world.

He is the *heart* of light and the *heart* of space. But that, which is the heart, is not awareness, is not consciousness, nor is it unconsciousness. It is That Which Is, as *this*. But, when you say "this is it," then this is *not* it! No matter where you point to, you create separation from something else.

There is no second, there is nothing but *This*. The light of the sun is not the sun. This is the principle, as in the example of water: it appears solid as ice, airy as steam, and liquid as water—but in its nature it's always water.

Consciousness, in all of its states of matter, is still consciousness. Its nature is not changed by the way it shows itself. Consequently, the nature of ignorance is also that which is knowledge.

What It Means, To Live In The Tao

You are that which is not findable.

When I really know what it means,
to live in the Tao,
then mostly going astray
is what I fear.

Questioner
Is it a story that one has a body in order to learn something?

Karl
Yes, yes. Sounds good. After all, "I am so important that I have to learn something so that I get to graduate at some point!" Wonderful. All these are the esoteric stories and fairy tales of this world!

Buddhists are always busy meditating in order to stop the wheel of reincarnation. The eightfold path, the possible—or impossible—meditations, right actions, all point toward stopping reincarnation. And how do you stop it? How can this be done? By not finding oneself in anything that is incarnated. Not-finding that which one is, in any kind of incarnation—neither physical nor spiritual, nor in the so-called awareness-incarnation. In the absolute not-finding, you are. You are that which is not findable in anything, whatsoever.

There has never been an incarnation. The complete stopping of the idea of being born finishes the wheel of reincarnation. It is always still, never turning. What has no existence can't turn.

There is the "experience" of being born, but in all the experiences of birth there has never been one who was born.

In not-finding an incarnated one, all incarnation comes to an end—but not so you don't have to come back again, not so you go into the *bardo* and a priest, sitting next to you, says "stay where you are, don't you come back, that's not the right thing for you."

After forty eight days you'll get fed up with it anyway. And what do you do next? You'll see two copulating ones and *zap*, you are back in it! Everything . . . all over again.

You think, "Let the priest babble whatever he wants. *There* is the music, *there* is the bachelor party, *there* is where it is happening! What does the priest want from me? He just wants to keep me in the nirvanic "whatever." There is nothing happening here; everything is just still. How boring."

Immediately, you return to where something is happening. No chance. You cannot separate yourself from that which you are.

When You Mold The World, Your Life Becomes Broad

And when I say you, I mean You.

When you mold the world,
your life becomes broad.
According to your world, judge the world of others.
How do I know the composition of the world?
Exactly through this.

Questioner
What I am, my being, does it exist?

Karl
It exists, because it doesn't exist. If it existed as a
"something," then it wouldn't be what it is.

Questioner
Abstraction was never my strength.

Karl
But that's just the point: to abstract. The abstract is
only the abstraction of what it is by taking away everything, and remaining as that which always remains.
But what remains can't be experienced. This is the
"non-experiencable-ness" of that which you are. Everything you can experience can be dropped, but not
"that which experiences."

And when I say you, I mean *You*. I always speak from
an absolute *I* to an absolute *You*. There is neither one
nor two; there is only Being, which knows neither one
nor two. Neither is there oneness. Being *is*, even if it
is two. Then it is two-ness, three-ness, four-ness, five-
ness, drunkenness, sobriety, beauty, or ugliness. Being
is Being, no matter which attributes it has. It remains
and is what it is. It doesn't need oneness, which would
already be "conditional" Being.

Majority, multiplicity, simplicity, complication. Being
remains Being.

He Who Lives Out Of His Origin's Fullness

Fear isn't anything bad!

He who lives out of his origin's fullness,
is like a newborn child.
It can scream all day long,
and yet it doesn't get hoarse:
Complete harmony!

Questioner
Do you know fear?

Karl
The body knows fear.

Questioner
Which body?

Karl
Here is this body-mind-mechanism.
If it had to jump from a 10-meter
tower, it wouldn't jump because it
would have fear. What's wrong with
that? Fear isn't anything bad. Who is
afraid of fear, and who needs it? Fear is an experience
within Being.

The infant doesn't have any problem with screaming.
It doesn't have any problem with being cold, hungry, or
afraid. It takes years to talk him into having a problem
with this or that. He first has to learn that something
is supposed to be avoided and another pursued. When
he learns this he has a problem, but that which he is,
never changed. Never does it for you, unless you have
a "problem" with having a problem. That's all. That's
the whole joke.

Until your third year, there is no sense of "my" body
or "my" toy. This information is just told to you. It's
second-hand information, which at some point, you
believe.

Questioner
Did you throw all your beliefs down the drain?

Karl
Yes, *pang*—a soap bubble burst.

Questioner
Did it feel good?

Karl
No, neither good or bad. You just *are*. Nothing ever happened to you. That which I am talking about is the most subtle "Aha" that sees nothing ever happens. It's nothing more.

It is total effortlessness to *be*. For this, nothing has to be added, nor is there anything to know. I don't even have to be aware of myself in order to be what I am. This is so natural; naturalness itself. It is prior to the idea of nature.

This is the peace that can never be disturbed by anything.

The One Who Knows Doesn't Speak

You are this silent smile.

The one who knows doesn't speak.
The one who speaks doesn't know.

One has to shut one's mouth
and close one's gates,
dull one's sharpness,
dissolve one's scattered thoughts,

dim one's light,
make one with earthly dust.
This is called primal union (with the Tao).

Yes, there is an inner smirking. One simply cannot kill it because it is smiling now, and has been forever.

It is always smiling in the background. It's grinning about the one who takes himself so importantly that he can't laugh about what is happening to him. You can't destroy this silent, friendly smiling in the background!

And it smiles especially when you think you could do something in order to reach it. This is the joke it likes most to hear. It plays this one all the time, whenever there is time. Really, you have no chance. Even when attempting not to push, your will itself is an attempt to push it. No chance.

And you—you are this silent smile. You are also the fidgeting someone who wants to do something, and also can't laugh about yourself.

You are helpless and you can't accept the helplessness. The next possible approximation is to "accept" that you cannot accept.

Through Not-Wanting,
One Wins A Kingdom

The source remains.

With intelligence, one leads an army.
Through not-wanting, one wins a kingdom.

As long as there is belief in a "me," there are two. And when there is belief in a "non-me," there are still two. The hope, the idea, that a me can remain that is without you, is absurd.

Consciousness happens to realize itself through self-exploration, or out of the existential crisis to want to know itself. This is its motivation. Thus, the source of all fears of this "little me" is simply this first awareness of existence.

This separate being doesn't start with the body but much earlier, with the first existential experience of being, of awareness. Because there is already someone who is aware of himself, there are two. This is the first idea of God—an awareness-God-and-Father—who becomes the root-idea. Everything else are just reflections, are effects of this first accident.

So, watch out for the beginnings! Or rather, go back to the beginning, to the first or last experienceable-ness, which is the root of all other experiences. Thus, "back" to the subject who first appears as "I"-awareness.

Then, the question will pose itself if the first subjective awareness has any reality. Finally, not even that one will pose itself—there will be no going back to the beginning anymore, no going back to the source.

The Sage Sharp, Without Cutting

*What comes and goes can't
be that which is knowledge.*

If a government is quiet and non-intrusive,
His people are sincere and honest . . .

The Sage is sharp, without cutting,
he is pointed, but not piercing,
he is genuine, but not unrestrained,
he is light, without blinding.

Questioner
Is the absolute Being beyond the eggshell that surrounds me?

Karl
It is neither "beyond" nor "here and now." The absolute Being is that which *is* the beyond, and it is also

that which is here and now. No matter what you say, or label it, it is "that which is," that you label. So if you say "it is the world," then it is not the world, but that which *is* the world. When you say "it is the body," then it is not the body, but that which *is* the body.

The nature of God is to be that which *is* God, but doesn't *know* itself as God. It isn't God, but that which is, as God.

The moment you become the definer you seemingly separate yourself from yourself, because the definer and the separation exist only in the definition. And that is not real. Nothing is ever separate. Nevertheless, you have the experience of separation, because no matter what you align yourself with, you take that for real.

Truth is in the omnipotence of your perception. And, if for you separation is reality, then the separation is the truth. This is the powerlessness of God. He is the Almighty, but he has no power.

You execute yourself the moment you experience yourself as relative object and experience it as truth. Then it is the truth to be a relative object, but it is God's truth. This is the execution of God—it's the only suicide that God can commit—to experience himself as relative object.

Questioner
With good conscience?

Karl
A bad conscience. *Geh-Wissen* is a German word for conscience, meaning "go knowledge." This is knowledge that comes and goes. Because the knowledge that you are this or that is not always permanent. Therefore, it cannot be that which *is* knowledge. The nature of knowledge must be, uninterruptedly, "that which is knowledge." What comes and goes cannot be that which is knowledge. It can be an aspect of it, but not the knowledge that you are longing for.

If Nobody Knows Our Limits

Waste the time you don't have.

If nobody knows our limits,
we can own the world.
If one owns the mother of the world,
one wins eternal duration.
This is the Tao of the deep root,
of the firm ground,
of the eternal Being
and of the enduring vision.

Waste the time you don't have, you have nothing to lose. Just try to waste the time that doesn't exist.

That's work. Or try "safe time," because you always think of hardship. You meditate in time, because it could get serious later.

It is beautifully crazy. That's *Ver-ruecktheit*—a German word for craziness, which literally means "moved over." You are moved over from something, which is your primordial state, into something crazy. That's the insanity. Because you are born, you have a sense of dwelling. You are so crazy that you try to find a home in some kind of circumstance. You are that crazy. Is that not crazy?

That's painful. *pain*-full. One needs a cam-*pain* or one becomes a *pain*-ter, an artist. To be an artist is the biggest torment; he is constantly in doubt about what he does. That's why it is called *pain*-ter—after the pain of creating. It's like a birth channel for Being, before he gets his thing out of there. Oh, language is great!

This is exactly the craziness: that you believe you are sometimes in and sometimes out. That's the sexual thing, to be in or out. When you are in you feel well, and when you are out you want to go back in again. So in this special circumstance, where you are apparently penetrating what you are, you *seem* to be "in"—but when you are out, then: "Oh! Quickly, back in!"

This is only two sides of the same coin of which you are. The coin has a peaceful, harmonious side, and also a disharmonious one. Both contain "harm."

You can't be one without the other, or else you would

have to cut off the side of you that doesn't fit: "This doesn't fit, I have to do *Vipassana* now." *Vipassana* is a Buddhist technique to practice attention. I change it to *wie passa mer*—a German play on words that means "how do we fit," how does it fit me. You always want to make things fit. That's the thing.

If One Governs The World According To The Tao

In deep sleep you don't know that you exist.

If one governs the world according to the Tao,
then the departed won't roam around as ghosts.

In deep sleep you don't know that you exist. Not in the sense of intellectual knowledge, nor in language, nor in images, nor in sensory impressions. And for what? This only interests you when the doubter is present. Where is the doubter in deep sleep? Where is this coward—that you believe to be here now—in deep sleep? Does the coward exist then? Are you afraid in deep sleep?

No? Just see. Then, you can say that your nature is fearlessness. It is not stirred up by anyone or anything.

Questioner
But I can't really be sure. How could I possibly know if I am afraid in deep sleep, when I am not aware of anything?

Karl
That's what I am saying: nobody cares. The "carer" only cares now, because he is awake. As soon as the carer is awake he starts to care about something: about how the carer is, whether the carer is still there in deep sleep, and on and on. But the carer can only care when he is awake. Otherwise, he doesn't even exist. There is no caring about what you are not, when there is no carer. Everything understood? Doesn't matter. Me neither.

Freedom is not fathomable. It is not controllable. No thought or feeling can touch it. There can be no attempt at grasping because there simply isn't anything graspable. It is, and remains, totally unfathomable. That is what you are: total fathomable-lessness. The wonder and joy to be that which is unfathomable.

If you were really fathomable you would be controllable, which would be prison. Then, you might as well kill yourself right away. But thank God you are not only un-graspable, but also un-conditionable and un-killable. The idea that you could "fathom" yourself is already hell, but the sense-lessness and non-findable-ness that you are, is total relaxation.

Just try to catch time! You can't find it. Time is the idea of two-ness—that the experiencer is separate from that which he experiences. It's the so-called separation of the seer from that which is seen. The idea that there is someone who could be bothered or seduced by anyone else is a burden one constantly carries around. It's the idea of being different from the world, of being vulnerable.

When you find out that you are the seer, the seeing, and the seen, then only Being remains. That which you are, life itself, which experiences itself as all of this, can't be hurt by its own nature. There is no danger, just total dangerlessness for that which you are.

The Feminine Always Prevails

Satiation is another word for Self.

In keeping downstream, a great kingdom
becomes the unification of the world.
It is the mother of the world.
The feminine always prevails,
through stillness, over the male.

The beauty of meditating is this: that as long as you have your eyes closed, you can't get into trouble. That's why I find meditating wonderful. At least during the time that there is peace.

Any type of meditation is a kind of drug. Whatever you try, and whatever you eat, is always a drug. Any kind of stimulation is always distraction. Even when you want to be satiated, it is a drug, because you reach a point of satiation. A psychological drug just creates another kind of satiation, but it can never make *you* satiated. Satiation is another word for Self. *Satt* is a German word for "'full," which is another word for Self. In Sanskrit, *Sat* means "Truth." The satiation that you are can never become satiated because it already is satiated

Has there ever been one second when you did not meditate in your Beingness? You are consciousness; you are that which *is* meditation. More is not possible; there is nothing else but meditation. If one calls it "sitting down" or "being quiet," it is just a certain method of meditating. Meditation is the action of consciousness without intention, without expectation of any result. This is here and now, has always been like this, and will always be so.

Here and now consciousness is absolutely active and reactive towards itself. This is the meditation of consciousness on itself. This will never come to an end, so you better enjoy yourself, because it will take a while.

The Tao Is The Home Of All Things

Outside is inside and inside is outside.

The Tao is the home of all things,
the good men's treasure,
the bad men's protection.

In America, you hear loudspeaker announcements at the airports: "Don't try to be funny in front of an officer. You may end up in a place you don't want to be." It means don't make fun of certain things or you may suddenly be stuck in a straitjacket.

That's what you are doing anyway, because you are crazy. As soon as you wake up, the craziness is there. You can't get out of it. The loony bin starts with the psyche. There is *Atman*, the original soul, which realizes itself. Psychiatry immediately starts, and with it the neuroses—or "old roses." But everyone wants "new roses." La vie en rose!

There is no escaping psychiatry; outside is inside and inside is outside. There's no path that leads you away from somewhere, nor is there any chance to reach somewhere else. Ramana called this "the surrender of the surrender, the giving up of the giving up!"

This is total resignation. It's the idea that you can

never leave that which you are, that remembrance
and surrender won't produce anything, because "who"
surrenders the surrenderer? That's the one you want
to surrender. "Who" or "what" packs the suitcase for
the hoper?

Who Practices Non-Doing

Every night the two-ness stops.

He who practices non-doing,
preoccupies himself with occupationlessness,
finds taste in that which doesn't taste:
he sees the big in the small and the many in the few.

Many have an idea of the "dark night of the soul" in
which we first have to experience the deepest suffering
in order to be fed up enough to resign completely, and
finally find peace. And, with the attitude, "If it will be
like this, then so be it. Everything is possible."

But you could also have it easier: simply be what you
are. That which you are you cannot *not* become, so just
be it.

There is no dark night of the soul for that which you
are. Whatever you imagine only exists as an idea.
Whether the phantom goes through a dark night of the

soul and suffers, or doesn't suffer, only makes a difference for the phantom. Only a phantom can become
enlightened, but who cares whether a phantom is
enlightened? Only the phantom and other phantoms.

Every night the folding chair folds away, and every
night the two-ness stops. Each moment in which the
experiencer disappears, you simply are—without perception—you just are.

Every morning the trap opens again, only this folding
chair wants to know whether he has an advantage,
whether he has to wait or not. Then you are waiting
for *Godot*, waiting for God. When does God come? God
never comes, God is here already. This is the problem:
God can't come, because more God is not possible.
Neither is less. And, where should God come from, or
go to?

You are here and now, with or without a sufferer or
carer. What you are *is* God.

Thank God.

Whoever Holds On, Loses It

Arunachala, even this light is still a dream.

A journey of a thousand miles
starts in front of your feet.
Whoever acts, spoils it.
Whoever holds on, loses it.

The timeless moment of the absolute sobering happened at the Arunachala mountain. Maybe that is why there is this gratefulness here, to not have to thank anyone to be what I am. Not even a mountain. Not even Louis Trenker, the famous German mountaineer. Nobody. I am what I am.

This mountain is considered to be the light of Shiva. The purest sense of Being, which presents itself as light. When you go into this mountain, in this heart cave, you really go with your perception. Then, as Ramana said, it is really like a vast landscape. You go inside it, and suddenly the mountain is pure light. Awareness-light.

And you know this from your own light. Light comes to light. You dissolve in this light, then a light turns on for you. You view *from* the light, as the original source of the universe. Each structure streams out of the light. Each nuance, each vibration, emerges out of this light, and forms itself into a structure of information;

of a universal star network or whatever. Whatever is, comes out of this stupid light.

Then, suddenly, you get it, "Shit, since you can still *perceive* the light, you cannot *be* the light—and even this light is still a dream. Shit!" You were so nicely at home in that light! Even the home of the light is a wrong home; you don't have a home, there is no home.

For what you are, there is no home. Jesus said, "I have no place where I can rest my head." There is no home for what I am. I can't come home; I can never be home. Never!

This could have happened anywhere, even on Christmas in front of the Christmas tree. But it happened there [Arunachala]. I am not the only lunatic who says that this mountain has special meaning. Apparently, existence arranges itself to say this mountain is special. Why not, then. It is a pointer, and a pointer is never that which it points to.

Mysterious Life Is Deep

It is all self-made.

Mysterious life is deep, far-reaching,
different than things;
but in the end it brings about the great harmony.

It is like in the waiting room of the doctor. There is a competition going on to determine who is sicker. With the enlightenment idea, it's "who is closer to enlightenment?" These Olympic games of existence are always going on. Who jumps the furthest? Who is the sickest? Who is the healthiest? Everyone competes to be either the smartest or the most stupid, depending on what is asked for. You have to observe this sometime. Two friends meet and immediately there is a competition: which girlfriend or which man is the best or worst. Apparently, this is the primordial tendency of Being, to be in competition, starting with Adam and Eve.

When you put God in the witness stand, it's you who sits there. You are the guilty one, because it is your own fault. Who else is there? It is all self-made. Of course you couldn't prevent it, because you are absolutely helpless, just like you can't prevent waking up.

Because that which you are woke up, it realized itself. You became a creator, and out of the creator came the act of creating, then the creation. Every morning, when you come out of the state of "statelessness," you wake up. Then, there is a creator who creates his world and puts it together—in both small and large things. And you are the small and the large.

It is really your own fault. This is realization: to realize that it is your own fault. At this point there is no more God, no father, and no family. There is nothing anymore that you must cope with because it is really your own fault. So you can no longer make anyone else responsible except that which one is. You are responsibility itself. This is being grown up—to be that which you are.

Because The Sage Doesn't Argue

There is only consciousness,
that plays everything.

 That streams and oceans are the kings of all rivers, comes from the fact,
that they can hold themselves low.
So does the Sage.
Because the he doesn't argue,
nobody in the world can argue with him.

It is only consciousness that plays everything. The perpetrator, the action, and the victim are all played by consciousness. Mr. Bush and Mr. Bin Laden, and everything you can imagine, is played by that, which is energy.

Questioner
So I can actually not decide anything?

Karl
You have been decided a long time ago. You have the experience of free will, but this doesn't mean that it is reality. Nevertheless, your experience makes you believe

that because of your decision something will happen. The experience is there, but the experience and the decision already happened prior to their perception. The problem is that you still have the illusion—the apparent experience—that you decided. This happens to be the way in which you realize yourself. You are the decider, the deciding, and that which you decide, but you cannot decide "what" you decide. You also cannot want what you want, *before* you want what you want.

That is all; that is peace. No one can want what he wants, not even God.

Just try to think *before* you think. Then, try to find the source where the first thought comes from. Try to want, *before* you want what you want. It doesn't work, it's impossible. You always arrive at something which is just a reaction to a previous action. Then you get to Adam and Eve, or to the amoeba, or to the big bang—or to the bang that you once had, which you always carry around with you.

So you never find the beginning of that which you are. Possibly, you can then recognize that this absolute potential now, this moment, carries all possible and impossible futures and pasts in itself. And it starts now and stops now, so that the beginning and end of Being is *here and now!* Absolutely! The big bang is always here and now!

You are identical with all the "banging," with that which is. Whenever you want that which is, you don't want anything, and if you want nothing, you want what is. You are free; you are will. This is absolute free will. This way you are the king, because you don't try to escape the primordial ground to rebel and rise yourself up over the primordial ground.

You simply are what you are. Where you don't want to escape, and don't rise up artificially, you rule. Because you rule anyway. Whether chaos rules, or peace and calm rule, it is always only you.

Only The One Is Great, Whose Greatness Doesn't Mean Anything To Him

The thinker is already a thought.

Only the one is great,
whose greatness doesn't mean anything to him.
Exactly because the Tao is big, it is useless.

The thinker is already a thought, but a thought that nobody can think of. You didn't get this? It doesn't matter. If you understood this, you wouldn't exist anymore. Then you would have "stood yourself up."

No cup can decide whether coffee or tea is poured into it, and no saucer can decide which cup is placed on it.

You are the absolute perpetrator and you never did anything. Nor will you ever do anything. You are the doer, the doing, and the done. This is the end of separation: you are the seer, the seeing, and the seen. You, the seer, is no longer separate from the seen. Or, as the actor from the action. You never were. You realize yourself as three different ones: as actor, as action, and as acted, but you are the *source* of all three. This is peace, because there is no second.

Peace cannot be gained. The peace that you are, you cannot *not* be—neither can you lose it or gain it. Peace, that one can "have," is illusion. To not be able to escape the madness you are is peace. The total hopelessness, to not be able to escape yourself, is peace. You are that which is, in all circumstances.

To realize yourself is madness. But you can't stop the madness, because wanting to stop the madness *is* madness. The craziness to want to make it healthy *is* craziness. To want to overcome your psychosis *is* psychosis.

To look for that which you already are is the psychosis. To be that which you are is the fulfillment. In nothing else you will be that, which is eternally fulfilled. Live life as life lives you. You can't separate one from the other.

Being In Accord With
The Way of Heaven

The eye of God.

He who leads well,
has no thirst for war.
He who fights well,
is not angry.
This is the virtue of noncontention;
this is being in accord with the Way of Heaven.

There is no proof that you exist at all. Even your birth video is no proof. There is something that slipped out, but what does this prove?

Since its beginning, all science tries to prove matter. At the moment this approach seems to be on shaky ground because quantum theory depends upon the perception of light appearing as a particle or wave. As a result, nothing can be proven.

That, which we have tried to prove, cannot be proven, because it needs the space and the time of the observer, which can't be found. This is where science stands at the moment—at "that which is"—namely, the eye of God.

That which is perception is undefinable and unproveable, because everything that can be proved exists in time and space.

But that which is the eye of God is prior to time and space, prior to the idea of being or non-being—and this cannot be proven.

Given this information, physicists and mathematicians become Buddhists or other spiritual seekers. Parapsychologists or Paraphysicists. I find this resignation of science to be wonderful. This resignation, alone, means freedom.

The freedom of the unknowableness of that which *is* freedom is the definition of freedom. This alone is freedom.

The most terrifying idea you should really be afraid of would be if science succeeded in finding you. Then, you would be an object in time and space.

The good news is that this "non-findeableness" is freedom. You don't exist as something findable. You will never *find* yourself. Not-finding yourself is the good news, not the finding of yourself.

The non-findeableness of a you, in time and space, means that you are prior to time and space, prior to the idea of coming and going, and altogether prior to any concept of existence.

This is the joyous message of medicine. The ultimate

medicine is the non-finding of a sick one. Is that not beautiful?

Walking Without Legs

You can never reach freedom.

Walking without legs,
fencing without arms,
throwing without attacking,
armed without using a weapon.

Actually, your tendency is simple: you want freedom. The idea of freedom lets you look for it, which is the prison. There, freedom becomes a prison. So you continue to cling to the idea and sit in detainment. There is no escape.

It is all detainment. As soon as you look, you are already in detainment. I always say that as soon as you are born, you automatically have a life-sentence and a death penalty on top of it. Then, you can do whatever you want—drinking, smoking, etc.—a little more dependency. Who cares? You can't escape it anyway!

So just die right away—recognize that you don't exist! You are the freedom you are looking for. You cannot be in detention. You cannot be found nor can you be lost, neither were you born nor will you die. You also cannot *not* be in detention—you are unconditionally conditional and unconditionally unconditional.

You can never reach freedom because if freedom was reachable it would be conditional. If that which is freedom was dependent upon circumstances, then freedom would be a circumstance itself, and it would be conditional and controllable.

You could fight wars over it and it would actually be effective. One could get something and lose something. How horrid!

My Words Are Very
Easy To Understand

Without thinking there is no "me."

My words are very easy to understand,
very easy to execute.
But no one on earth can understand them,
can execute them.

You want to feel what you are? Then you become a track hound. There is no reason not to. One calls it "watchdog-being." Always watchful. Each movement, every little hair is watched—what I do right now and how I wake up. Shortly before getting up I am *already* there. To always be awake. Always the watchdog. I am so awake. I am so close to myself, I almost feel myself.

Questioner
But there are moments in which one perceives oneself more than usual.

Karl
During orgasm? When both melt together, and there is no one there anymore, then you feel yourself the most because you don't *feel* yourself. This is the climax: one absolutely doesn't feel oneself anymore because there is no one there. The feeling of two is totally gone in orgasm. One doesn't feel oneself at all. This is the climax of being, just like in deep sleep.

So, you've got to do what you've got to do. You go to bed with another because you don't want to feel yourself. As long as you feel yourself there is always something wrong. During orgasm one is totally absorbed in perception, and in the exuberance of all this energy one is not there as an experiencer. This is called "climax." It's the absence of me—it's the little death. And again and again, up and down, so one is gone.

In the aerobics of "I"-lessness, one fights with oneself as if there are no others in an infinite competition—it's one player who plays all of the rolls in the Olympic game of life.

Here, one laughs oneself to death. In fact, everyone comes to me to laugh themselves to death. Others may cry themselves to death, which is the same thing, because during laughing and crying one can't think. And without thinking there is no "me."

Who Knows Of His Not-Knowing

If I understood what I am saying . . . my goodness!

He who knows of his not-knowing,
out of him the nobility of the spirit shines.
He who doesn't know of it, is tangled in delusion.

To "become like little children" simply means to throw out all this shit of experience—the world-wisdom, and little treasures—that you carry around with you, in the realization that they are worth nothing. They are already gone.

You don't get anything out of it anyway, so just amuse yourself in the search for them, and enjoy yourself in the search. Or, be glad that you don't get any understanding, because you can't have it anyway. Thank God!

The babbling idiot here, on the speaker's platform, is supposed to understand this? He can talk about it, but he doesn't know what he is talking about. If I understood what I am saying . . . my goodness!

But something always understands. This is strange for the "understander"—when he stands next to it—because that one always mis-stands himself. He just stands around stupidly, never understanding anything, anyway. If you only leave that one out of it, then it speaks by itself, it understands by itself.

If you don't get this now, then okay; the "me" doesn't understand it anyway. But you'll notice that something in you understood it completely, naturally. There isn't even a question of "not-understanding" or the "need-to-understand." There is total questionlessness . . . or not.

Then the doubter, the one who wants to understand, immediately begins to doctor around again. That's his nature. What to do to stop it? He always starts to grumble and to ruminate, again.

Just let him grumble. The phantom immediately needs to doubt: "was this it, was it not it? Is this it now?" Hah, it never stops!

Doesn't matter though. The natural understanding, which is what you are, doesn't care whether you are delusion or nobility of spirit, or even whether you know of your "not-understanding."

Don't Interfere In Their Homes

Ashrams should actually be called "reeperbahn"
(a red light area in Hamburg).

If the people have no sense of awe,
there will be disaster.
Don't interfere in their homes
or burden their lives.
Only by not wearying them,
they will not be weary of you.

You always only love yourself, and you always only refer to yourself. Your dilemma is just that you forgot yourself.

If you turn toward yourself as that which you are, prior to the questioner and all questions, you are free. But as long as you confuse yourself with any characteristics or states, your narcissism is directed only to them.

There is, in fact, nothing but narcissism. Every movement is narcissistic. It's an ancient tradition. Hitler didn't invent it, the ego is always a Nazi. It always knows better than existence, how existence needs to be—currently, 6.5 billion times in this world. Even babies already know what is better: "The breast should be nice and big, which is better than small," so that it can feed well. Is that where everything starts: who has the biggest breast? Or not.

Questioner
But people didn't volunteer to go to a concentration camp, whereas in an Ashram they do.

Karl
You think!

Questioner
But there nobody is forced.

Karl
You have no idea. Consciousness starts by picking you, who is hanging out totally depressed at home, thinking: "The ashram is my only salvation." You just hope that you can breathe again. That's pure tyranny. Consciousness will take you there, whether you want to go or not.

You don't go voluntarily, only out of the hope that you will be better off after you sit properly and look inside. Or, when you seemingly volunteer to clean the latrines—many, many times—in the service of the master.

Even for enlightenment, you hope, "The master will do me the right way, so that when I come, it will be the last time."

Ashrams should actually be called "*reeperbahn*" (a red light area in Hamburg), because they raise hopes.

73

The Sage Doesn't Waver

You are *meditation.*

The Sage doesn't waver,
and still everything comes by itself.
He is unperturbed
Yet still good at planning.
Heaven's net is quite wide-meshed,
but it doesn't lose anything.

A seeker sits down and meditates, closes his eyes, and thinks that by not-doing he will get something: "I am doing nothing right now, then I will get something for it. At least I'll get a little bit of peace. But for that I have to sit still." Then he is in the Grandprix of Eurovision, where the song *A Little Peace* won the European song competition on TV. A big prize!

But you cannot *not* meditate; your nature *is* meditation. You are meditation, you are consciousness, and you meditate infinitely.

This special meditating, this sitting down, is an aspect of meditation, but it is nothing special. There is nothing wrong with it, but there is also nothing right either, because you can only meditate and not do anything else. But I am against this special meditating. To say, "I have to do this and that, and only through a particular way can I reach such-and-such. . . ." Who decides that? Who sets the standards?

Any moment in which you perceive yourself and realize yourself, you meditate on that which you are. Meditation is exploration; it's an infinite self-exploration. There is no moment without meditation, because where there is a moment, there is time. Where there is time, there is realization. Where there is realization, you are. You *are* meditation.

Your nature is meditation. Existence knows best what there is to do, and how to meditate, so that it experiences an "Aha" at a certain point: "Ah, I am that. For that which I am, nothing ever happened, anyway."

Existence knows best. "Who" says what is better or worse? I have no idea. I also don't say, "You should not meditate." I only say, "No one knows what is good or bad, or what will happen."

I can only point out that you are, in each moment, that which meditates.

There Is Always A Death
Force Which Kills

The train drives by itself.

There is always a death force which kills.
To kill in place of this death power is
as if one wanted to swing the ax
in the place of the carpenter.
Whoever wants to swing the ax
instead of the carpenter,
rarely escapes
without hurting his hand.

Everything one can imagine, no matter how bizarre or
natural, is a loony bin, a theater of the absurd. Every
day is the great performance! Endlessly. It's like a
job interview: once you start to have a conversation
with yourself you are in an interview—then, there is
already two—so you introduce yourself to yourself.
Because who can have a conversation by himself?

But you can't introduce "you" to yourself, no matter
how well you may describe yourself. The whole of existence is a description of yourself, and it isn't worth a
thing. It doesn't strike you, because it can't touch you.
It can't even be tangent to you peripherally, because
you don't have a periphery. Apart from "you," nothing
is. And you are nothing. Is it not beautiful?

You are always afraid that there is something you can't control, that something could happen that you don't want. You are afraid to lose the control that you don't have. But your body is always set on auto-pilot. Your feeling. Your thinking. Everything. The train drives by itself.

It is the death experience, the experience of totality, which doesn't need to experience itself in order to be. It is total, but without experience. What was the experience of Jesus in the resurrection? Where did he go, to the dead? Or, into totality, into Beinglessness. He experiences, in Beinglessness, that which he doesn't have to be in order to *be*. This is the experience of life: to be that which *is* life—to be that which doesn't need an "experience" of life in order to be life itself. This is eternal life, which is never-never.

And this eternal life is also in the death experience of life. This is the experience of being "that which is life," where there is no fear of death, because there isn't any death.

Like in deep sleep. Here we are again.

(75)

He Who Doesn't Act For The Sake Of Life

The message of inconsolableness.

The people make light of death,
because the rulers strive to live extravagantly;
this is why they make light of death.
But he who doesn't act for the sake of life
is better than him to whom life is precious.

I know that you want consolation, but "who" needs
this consolation? Precisely, this inconsolableness is
here and now, which is the very message. If there *is*
a message, then it is the message of inconsolableness.

There can't be an end, because it never began. As long
as you are, you suffer. Nothing ever stops. What doesn't
have a beginning can't have an end, even though you
dream of it. In the same way that you dream to be here
and to live, you dream to find an end in dying. You
were never born; you can never die.

That, of which I speak, can never be reached in time
and space; it can never be experienced in time and
space. This insight one cannot have because no one
can get there.

What you are is here and now, not a future event.
Nothing *can* happen, because for that which you are

nothing ever happens. Even in dying, there will be no moment of grace.

The Soft Ones And Weak Ones Are Companions Of Life

Who needs the concepts of "moment" and "now?"

When man enters life,
he is soft and weak,
and when he dies,
he is hard and strong.
This is why the hard and strong ones
are companions of death,
the soft and weak ones
companions of life.

That which you are is infinite—it never started and will never end. Equally infinite is the realization, in this world of appearances, that there is no beginning and no end, nor is there any escape. There is no one who is within and there is no one to emerge from it.

Questioner
There is no infinity because the idea of time is nonsense and because we always live in the moment.

Karl
Who is supposed to be living in this moment? Who needs the concepts of "moment" and "now?" Who is in this "power of now," and who needs it?

Questioner
Yes, okay, so I can just throw the concepts back in your face as well.

Karl
Yes, these are all concepts. This is exactly the possible and impossible—the possibility that you walk out of here free of concepts, is there, but not that you would leave with a better concept. One is no better than the other, because they both can't be true. Once you see that you are not here because of the concepts, but despite the concepts, it may cause you to stick your finger into your throat and throw them up all at once.

So, as long as you are chewing on concepts, then keep chewing. Grind them to an undefinable slime-ball, in which you can no longer find anything. This is freedom from construction and deconstruction. In this way, nothing is left for you. You are the absolute leftover, the remains, who has nothing, and no choice left. But *you* always remain. You are always that which is the absolute substratum. If you subtract everything that can be subtracted, you remain. You don't get to go any-where. This is called "abstractum."

The Sage Acts And Doesn't Keep

Does anything make you more or less?

Who is able to offer that to the world
which he has too much of?
Only he, who has the Tao.

The Sage acts and doesn't keep.
When the work is done, he does not rest in it.
He doesn't desire to show his significance in front
of others.

That which experiences itself, doesn't become more or
less through the way in which it experiences itself.

In this way, there is a development from one point to
another, but there is no one who changes in that which
he is.

So, does anything make you more or less? This is cru-
cial. Whether you experience yourself or don't experience yourself, or how you experience yourself, doesn't
make a difference. You are totally detached from the
manner of your existence.

There is no added value. You have to pay value added
tax, but you don't get anything for it. Meditation is
a value added tax. I may meditate, but I don't get
anything out of it. Beautiful things, hobbies, these are

fun. It's the fun factor. But there is no inherent quality except to do it for fun. But fun is not worth more or less than pain or boredom, nor do you become more or less through the experience of fun, pain, or boredom.

The next sip of coffee is not worth less than the highest experience of enlightenment. There is, moment to moment, always a different manner of experience—but through this you don't change. The highest experience doesn't make you more, nor will the most trivial experience make you less.

It Can't Be Changed By Anything

You are always your own judge.

In the whole world,
there is nothing softer and weaker than water.
And yet, in the way it attacks the hard,
nothing equals it.
It can't be changed by anything.
That the weak overcomes the strong
and the soft overcomes the hard,
everyone on earth knows,
but nobody is able to act accordingly.

You think of your actions and weigh whether they were right or wrong. Then, you may believe it is possible to do the right thing next time, or to avoid the wrong one. For that, you first must judge what has happened already. Thus, you are always your own judge, always in court with yourself. Madness.

This is "Judgment Day." It is always there—the eternal judge who goes to court with himself—the judge who has constant doubts about what he did, always asking himself what the meaning is of all that happens.

And if you suffer from it, then so what? And if you feel guilty, then so what? There is no one else here who did this to you; you alone are guilty. Totally innocently of course.

There is no God, no parents, no neighbors, no circumstance, which you can blame for being what you are and how it is. You are the primordial ground of all Being. More guilt is not possible.

This is the peace of "no way out." You mostly suffer because you don't accept it. But not because you are guilty. You are guilty, anyway—guilty of not accepting that you suffer from it. Then you become the poor sufferer, the one who pities himself. Unfortunately, the sufferer is always "one too many."

This is the absolute innocence, the total virginity of your nature. Nobody can bring this to you, nor can anyone take it away. You are it.

Circumstances will never be perfect enough for there to be peace. Thank God! Just imagine, that peace could be "created." Then, you would be dependent on a peaceful state. What kind of peace is it that needs a peaceful state!

The Sage Doesn't Demand Anything From Others

The whole of existence is the hobby of Being.

If one reconciles a great dispute
and still a grudge remains,
how can this be beneficial?
This is why the Sage sticks to his duty
and doesn't demand anything from others.

Up to a certain point, everyone always wants to love, there is the intention of love. But when it doesn't get fulfilled love can turn into hatred. Then one becomes a seeker. No one seeks himself in order to embrace himself. Actually, everyone would want to kill himself if he found himself.

When seeking begins you don't find happiness in the world, and there starts the hate—at least for the seeking. You want to *stop* seeking. Out of the intention of love becomes an intention of hatred. But even that is an intention of love.

You want to get rid of the relative love so that you can

have absolute love, which finally unchains you from the need to seek.

The hatred is also love, because one hates out of love. It is crazy: There is always love coming around—take *Reeperbahn*, which is the red light district in Hamburg—and going astray is fun. This is the orbit, the eclipse. If you always walk straight, you'll get to it. But, you first ride the roller coaster. This is like a hobby. One could say, the whole of existence is the hobby of Being. Out of this hobby it realizes itself. The little hobbit. The Self is the little hobbit with the big hobby.

And this is indeed great joy, yet it brings absolutely nothing. This is called fun. One doesn't have fun in order to gain something; fun is fun for its own sake.

If you could really reach something through enlightenment, it would be like a business deal with yourself: "When I have worked enough, I will finally get the payment of enlightenment, and then I will love myself. I will pay myself with love. I like paying myself. Then I will be so clear and pure that my body, my spirit, and my whole being shines. Then I can finally love myself. Finally, I am worth it to be what I am. So, I'll put upon myself one condition of how I should be so that I can love myself—as an enlightened one—because before I was not lovable enough."

You will never reach the state where "Nothing bothers me anymore, where there is nothing unlovable anymore. Everything is only lovable now, there is only love left and nothing but love." This doesn't work.

Because you want it, you want to bite into your own tail—and that one is so atrophied in human beings that you don't have a chance to start with. How do you want to reach there, anyway?

Let The People Take Death Seriously

*There is no blood that comes out of
that which is life.*

Let the people take death seriously
and not travel far.
Even if there were ships and carriages,
there should be no one who rides in them.

If Jesus was the savior then he was the savior from the evil idea of salvation. This was his crucifixion. He was the savior from the idea of salvation, because he showed that you can never be redeemed from that which you are.

So the pointer of the crucifixion is this: to be nailed horizontally to the temporal, nailed vertically to the spirit, then the spear comes and directly pierces the heart taking any idea of heart away from you.

This is a wonderful example of the inevitability of Being, where the heart is pierced, at the last, so that it bleeds out.

And the symbol tells us that everything is bleeding out. Every idea becomes bloodless, empty of life. Because no idea can hold itself in that which is life. And the eternal life doesn't *know* heart, and it doesn't *know* love, and it doesn't know anything that could remain.

And then you recognize: "My God. Now, even you have forsaken me!" Then you realize: "Even God can't help anyone, because there is no God." And then only heart remains. To the heart, nothing else remains but to be that which remains. But it doesn't *know* any heart.

There is no blood that comes out of that which is life. One can't kill it, it is eternal. That, which can be killed—this is the symbolism—cannot be that which is eternal life.

Jesus returns again from the totality, from the dead. He awakens from the totality of Being into something, which is *this*, and becomes absolute awareness, absolute spirit, and absolute man—but only in the last forty days. Or, was he already it before? I would say, he was it before and after, in between, and still is. Because that, which Jesus is, in his essence, is that which is here and now.

True Words Are Not Beautiful

I can only show you my own helplessness.

True words are not beautiful,
beautiful words are not true.
Proficiency doesn't persuade,
Persuasion is not proficient.
The Sage is not scholarly,
the scholar is not wise.
The Heaven's Tao furthers without harming.
The Sage's Tao operates without arguing.

I actually try to speak nonsense half of the time, so that you really don't get the impression that there is something to understand. Even cracking the most stupid jokes, so that no one gets the idea that someone is sitting here with something to say. But it doesn't help at all.

I can't give it to you; I can't take it from you; you are it, no matter what. You are always that, which always remains, and therefore nothing remains for you. So be it!

Be that which you cannot *not* be. Everything else is hocus-pocus. I can only keep repeating to myself, "Look, it isn't that bad; it is much worse. But it doesn't matter."

I can only show you my own helplessness. I can't give you anything or take away anything. Peace is always there, in a way that it is not even seen anymore. I can only point to it.

This peace is imperturbable. It won't come through being silent or talking. The idea that a relative me could create *this*—impossible, nobody can exist there. This is the coldest burn that you can get. No one cares whether you exist or not, whether you understand something or not. Whatever enlightenment experiences you have had doesn't even interest a dog. To think that Being would need enlightenment from this fart here. What an idea!

You know absolutely that you can never reach that which you are. But you still try—and it doesn't matter. You cannot make a mistake. You don't do anything in any case. Nor does it matter, anyway.

About The Author

During the 1990s Karl Renz encountered a moment of clarity in which there was no desire to change anything or to avoid pain or suffering. He felt, "If I must remain in this condition for the remainder of my existence, so be it." Karl later described it this way:

> "At that moment there was an absolute acceptance of being. Time stopped. Karl and the word disappeared and a kind of 'Is-ness' in a glaring light appeared—a pulsating silence, an absolute aliveness that was perfect in itself—and I was that."

Karl travels throughout the world sharing with spiritual seekers. He doesn't give instruction in a traditional way, but his paradoxical logic works brilliantly to help the mind relax, to let go of its grasping and seeking, so that we may recognize the changeless, absolute freedom that is our true nature.

To find out more about Karl's schedule, and to view some of his artwork, please visit his website at: www.KarlRenz.com

Aperion Books
Book Publishing for the Digital Age

Aperion Books is dedicated to producing high quality publications that help people facilitate positive change in their lives. We specialize in publishing titles on spirituality, wellness, and personal growth.

Our unique Collaborative Publishing Program is specifically designed to help writers and authors expand their personal and professional horizons through creatively designed books that are distributed to national wholesalers and leading retailers.

CPSIA information can be obtained
at www.ICGtesting.com
Printed in the USA
LVOW12s0203160418
573607LV00002B/116/P